"Appealing and handsome.... *Young Jane Austen* is a
thoroughly researched and credible representation of Jane
Austen's life from infancy through age twelve. This
lovely, delightful biography is a wonderful choice for all
Janeites wanting to learn more about Jane Austen's
childhood." –Austenesque Reviews

"*Young Jane Austen* is breathtaking. The writing is superb,
the illustrations brilliant, and the design gorgeous. I
especially enjoyed the book's focus on creativity and its
development. Glorious! Jane Austen would be proud!"
–Leslie McGuirk, bestselling author, artist, and creator of the
"Quest for Inspiration" workshops

"A charming book, daintily produced." –*Jane Austen's Regency
World*

"Delightful and infinitely readable.... I was impressed with
[Pliscou's] ability to take vast volumes of Austen scholarship and research and distill those down into a series of
very clear, very digestible paragraphs that really helped to
illuminate Austen's life story." –Austenprose

"A charming book, of interest to readers of all ages in its
imaginative retelling of central events in Austen's life and
its exploration of questions over which she must have
puzzled." –Sarah Emsley, author of *Jane Austen's Philosophy of
the Virtues* and *Jane Austen and the North Atlantic*

"A delightful glimpse into the world of the young Jane Austen, which will appeal to adults as well as teenagers. The narrative is beautifully written, enabling the reader to vividly imagine Jane's world of family, events, and her inner life, on the journey to becoming a writer during her formative years. The addition of annotations and reference material, gained from many sources, help further explore the historical background and context, along with accompanying illustrations, setting Jane Austen firmly in the Georgian world. A charming tribute." –Jane Odiwe, author of *Searching for Captain Wentworth* and *Lydia Bennet's Story*

"Delightful." –Savvy Verse and Wit

"Readers will be inspired to take on some of Austen's novels after reading this book.... The beautiful paper and illustrations of this book made me wish that more books were creatively printed. I felt as if I was reading a text from the time period of Austen's life, which made me feel warm and fuzzy.... The text begs for readers to conduct research." –Ricki Ginsberg, Unleashing Readers

"Like the very best of books, *Young Jane Austen* exists well beyond labels. It is an empathetic biography and an empathic search, a reflection on a singular person and an engaging, universal treatise on creative fervor. At the heart of it all lives an against-the-odds heroine who helped launch that strange, imperfect, necessary creature we now call the novel." –Beth Kephart, author of *Handling the Truth: On the Writing of Memoir* and *Going Over*

Young Jane Austen
BECOMING A WRITER

Also by Lisa Pliscou

Higher Education
Dude
David's Discovery

Young Jane Austen

BECOMING A WRITER

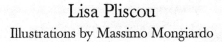

Lisa Pliscou

Illustrations by Massimo Mongiardo

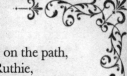

For my mom Peg, who started me on the path,
and for my mother-in-law Ruthie,
who loves books too
– LP

To my parents, for always being supportive of my art
– MM

F I R S T   E D I T I O N

ISBN: 978-1-939388-90-5
Library of Congress Control Number: 2014956539

The illustrations were rendered in brush pen on Bristol paper.
Book design by Nancy Cleary.

www.WyattMacKenzie.com

Publisher's Cataloging-in-Publication data

Pliscou, Lisa.
    Young Jane Austen : Becoming a Writer / Lisa Pliscou ; illustrations
by Massimo Mongiardo.
    pages cm
    ISBN 978-1-939388-90-5
    Includes bibliographical references and index.

1. Austen, Jane, 1775-1817 —Childhood and youth. 2. Novelists,
English —19th century —Biography. 3. England —Social life and
customs —18th century. I. Mongiardo, Massimo. II. Title.

PR4036 .P55 2015
823.7 —dc23   2014956539

Wyatt-MacKenzie Publishing
DEADWOOD, OREGON

CONTENTS

Introduction. vii

Young Jane Austen

Jenny 1

In the Village 5

Home. 9

Patterns. 13

Play. 17

Evening 21

Sunday 25

Words Dancing 29

Changes 33

The Writer of the Family 37

Leaving Home 41

School 45

Endings 49

Books. 53

The Abbey School 57

Cousin Eliza 61

The Dressing Room 65

Reading 69

Something New 73

Beginnings 77

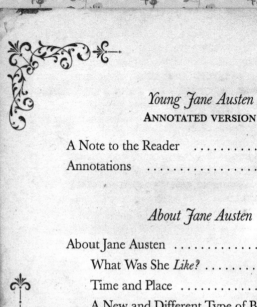

Young Jane Austen
ANNOTATED VERSION

A Note to the Reader 82

Annotations 83

About Jane Austen

About Jane Austen 139

    What Was She *Like?* 142

    Time and Place 144

    A New and Different Type of Book 147

    Jane Austen, Author 149

Timeline........................... 153

Sources 157

About the Illustrations 161

Acknowledgements 162

About the Author and Illustrator.......... 163

Index 164

INTRODUCTION

Facts and truth really don't
have much to do with each other.
WILLIAM FAULKNER

But history, real solemn history, I cannot be interested
in . . . a great deal of it must be invention.

CATHERINE MORLAND
in Jane Austen's *Northanger Abbey*

s these two quotes suggest, there can sometimes be an ambiguous line between fiction and nonfiction. In his provocative book *Reality Hunger,* David Shields asserts that no such line really exists — it's *all,* he says, fiction.

So where is the line, if any, in this book?

In *Young Jane Austen* I have written what might be called "speculative biography." Very little — so *very* little! — is known about Jane Austen as a young girl, but in utilizing a wide array of sources I've constructed a narrative that I hope encompasses, to paraphrase William Faulkner, both facts and truth. And I've added an annotated version of the narrative which features brief quotations from these sources (including Austen's books and correspondence), background details, ruminations on creativity, and connections to Austen's work as a mature writer which I found intriguing – the underpinnings, so to speak, of the construction process.

As for the speculative aspect: in trying to answer for myself the fundamental mystery of Jane's childhood and her astonishing development as a writer, it seemed most interesting to me to frame much of the narrative as if through the consciousness of a child. And as many of her biographers have done, I've drawn upon my sources – you'll find them identified in both the annotations and in a section at the back of the book – to adopt an interpretive approach in writing about young Jane's experiences during these first, eventful, powerfully formative years of her life.

Without this approach, *Young Jane Austen* would have been merely a brief list of the few facts that are generally agreed upon – and largely devoid of any sense of a living, breathing, wholly fascinating girl, whose future as a gifted artist was by no means assured.

It may be, then, that I have set a foot in both camps, thus satisfying neither the most stringent biographer nor the reader anticipating a great deal of dialogue and description. But there you have it. As Austen herself once cheerfully wrote, "Let other pens dwell on guilt and misery."

Here is my recreation of young Jane Austen's world.

— LISA PLISCOU
Gold River, California

Imagination is the beginning of creation.
You imagine what you desire,
you will what you imagine,
and at last you create what you will.

GEORGE BERNARD SHAW

Childhood is a novelist's whole capital.

LOUIS AUCHINCLOSS

Young Jane Austen

Jenny

*H*er story began long ago, in 1775, in a tiny village in England.

After weeks of gray fog and chilly rain, a day came that was, at last, brightened by the sun. On this day, to the Austen family was born a little girl, Jane. Everyone called her Jenny.

Slow months of bitter cold and heavy snows followed. But Jenny was warm and snug upstairs, sometimes held close to Mrs. Austen in her big soft bed, sometimes sleeping in a cozy cradle. The family tiptoed in and out, grateful that Mrs. Austen came safely through the birth, thankful for a baby that was healthy and strong.

In the Village

inter let go its fierce hold; icy snowdrifts melted into floods that turned the rough roads into a sea of slippery mud. Jenny was taken to Nanny Littleworth's cottage in the village. Like the other Austen babies, here she was to live until she reached what Mrs. Austen called the *age of reason* — when she could walk and say a few words and do some simple things for herself.

How strange to leave the big house where she had been born! But Nanny kept little Jenny safe and clean and dry. People came and went. As the months went by, they became familiar to her.

The tall man with the smiling eyes — that was *Papa*. And the short, slender lady who came bustling in to hug her, exclaim over her, then swiftly disappear — that was *Mama*. And five great big boys: Jemmy, George, Henry, Neddy, Frank. These were her brothers. And best of all, a girl-child, a sister – Cassy.

Jenny realized that although she lived *among* the Littleworths, she was not *of* them.

Home

One day, Jenny was taken back to the big house. Mama had told Cassy that she was to be a little mother to Jenny, so Cassy took her by the hand and showed her everything: the bedroom the two girls would share, Papa's study, the dining parlor where they ate, the sitting room, the kitchen where they mustn't bother Cook, and more. *This is home,* Cassy told her. *This is where you'll stay forever.*

It was all very different from Nanny's cottage. So many people, so many rooms! Loud, laughing boys thundering up and down the stairs, Papa coming and going, Mama seeming to be everywhere at once. The house was filled from morning till night with talking, footsteps, laughter. Noises. Words. Always words.

Jenny clung tightly to her big, kind sister.

Patterns

Day by day, Jenny came to know the shape, the pattern, of her new life.

In the morning, there was breakfast. At the big table were Papa and Mama and Jemmy and Henry and Neddy and some other boys who *weren't* her brothers. They were Papa's students who lived here, too. Jenny's place was at a little table with Cassy and Frank.

After, she would help Cassy, as best she could, with chores. Sometimes Mama sat with Cassy and Frank and taught them letters and numbers. But not for very long, for Mama was busy. She was in charge of the housekeeping: the cooking, the cleaning, the laundry, the sewing. She told the servants what to do. And she was in charge of the vegetable garden, the fruit orchard, the poultry yard, the beehives, and the dairy, too. Baking and brewing, churning and weeding, plucking and picking, feeding and mending – there was always so much to do.

Meanwhile, Papa taught the boys in his study, and he also oversaw the family's farm, which lay up the hill just beyond the village. He rode his horse there every day, to see the crops and the animals and to talk with the people who worked for him. How very tall he looked in the saddle!

The family gathered again for dinner, and afterwards Papa would read to his students: it might be a story about strong heroes and strange monsters, or about a poor sailor shipwrecked on a faraway island, or about a brave boy who pulled a sword from a stone and learned he was to be king.

Always it was *boys* who were clever and strong and brave.

Play

*A*fter, there was time for play. Outside was best, if the weather would let you. You could roll down the hill at the back of the garden. You could get your fingers wet in the pond. You could join a wild game of cricket or blind man's bluff. You could run along the lane, and see the pigs at the farm. You could go to the big barn and pretend you were a king or a monster or a sailor on a tossing ship, and be as loud as you liked – even if you were a girl.

Evening

As the day wound down, the family came together again, this time in the sitting room. Candles were lit, Mama took up her sewing, and Papa read out loud. Sometimes it was more stories. Sometimes it was the Bible. Or the newspaper, with reports of England, India, the troubled Colonies across the great ocean. Papa might read poetry, or plays. Sometimes it was letters from relatives all over the country, or even further away: from Germany, France, the West Indies, distant, mysterious places.

But Papa wasn't the only one whose voice was heard. Mama would often comment in her quick, clever way. The boys joined in, trying to outdo each other in wit and brilliance. Jokes, ideas, laughter flew back and forth. The Austens loved to make fun of *everything*.

Then the day was over. It was a happy, drowsy time with Cassy: prayers said out loud, secrets shared, quiet giggles, and, at last, sleep.

Sunday

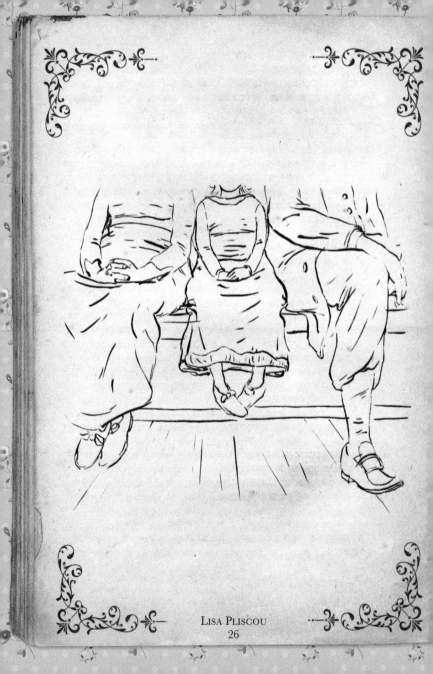

*S*unday was a special day, different from all the rest. In the morning and in the afternoon, the family walked up the steep hill to the gray stone church, where Papa would stand in the front and talk. For not only was Papa a teacher and a farmer, he was also the rector, helping everyone learn about God and to be better.

You had to sit very still and be very quiet and listen hard.

Jenny hardly knew what Papa was saying — she heard words like *sacrifice, resurrection, salvation; zeal, wrath, righteousness; meek, blessed, compassion* — but the syllables rolled off his tongue almost like a poem, solemn and important, that was wonderful to hear. Still, sometimes her feet got very cold.

Words Dancing

The days came and went. The seasons ebbed and flowed, each with its own pleasures and hardships, and twice each year Papa's students arrived and left for home. Life ticked on as steady as a clock. You knew what to expect, every day, every month, and you knew what was expected of you. Mama made sure of that.

But change, like a stone you tossed into the pond, rippled the smooth surface of things.

You got bigger and taller and could do more.

Jenny could dress herself — mostly. She was getting better at helping Cassy and Mama with chores. She was learning how to sew. And she had a book of her very own, which she looked at every day; it was easier than the books in Papa's study. It was about a girl who, though poor, was very good, and had many adventures and in the end was rewarded for her goodness and was married.

Jenny studied the pictures. She knew all the letters and could read *many* of the words by herself. She whispered them out loud, just to hear the sounds they made. *Dog. Cow. Good. Poor. Pudding. Basket. Happy. Pretty.* Words danced inside her head.

Changes

The family was changing, too.

A new baby, Charles, was born. Now Jenny could be a little mother along with Cassy, running to Nanny's to hold him and play with him.

Jemmy – who wanted to be called James now – left for a faraway city called Oxford, where he was to learn many things at the college and become a great scholar and a rector, like Papa.

Neddy – Edward – went on a long journey, traveling with their cousins Mr. and Mrs. Knight.

And George, who had fits, who could neither speak nor hear, would never, Mama said, reach the age of reason, and so he was sent to live with a kind family who would take care of him, in a village far away. Mama said they must be *rational* and they must *accept*.

But Jenny puzzled over this.

Cassy — usually so wise and knowing — had been wrong. Home was *not* a place where you stayed forever: although James would come back, for visits, and Edward would return from the Knights, George had been put somewhere else. They might see him sometimes, but he would never come home.

Poor George.

Yet life went on, steady as a drumbeat. Duties and chores, games and romps, secrets with Cassy and Charles' first steps, letters coming and letters going, words and books, Papa reading and Mama sewing.

The Writer of the Family

LISA PLISCOU
38

hristmas was always a delightful time, but this year brought a fascinating new delight. James was home, and announced that he and his brothers and their friends were going to put on a play! It was a thrilling story called *Matilda*, and James even wrote a new beginning and ending for it.

How exciting to watch the rehearsals, lively with laughter and squabbles. And what fun to finally sit in the dining parlor and see the actors, splendid in their costumes, saying their lines so well — and to be spellbound by the tale of murder and swordfights, trickery and true love, as it unfolded before your eyes!

Everyone told James how much they liked what he had written and made a great fuss over him, and about the essays and poems he had been composing, too, which he had been reading aloud to the family in the evenings. Mama declared that he was the writer of the

family. It was as if, Jenny thought, he had pulled a sword from a stone. Or, rather, a pen from a stone.

And could there be only *one* writer in a family?

Mama wrote letters – many letters – and also very funny, clever verses.

Papa wrote letters as well, and the sermons which he gave on Sunday.

Weren't they writers too?

It was something else to puzzle over.

Leaving Home

There was never enough money, it seemed, and in the spring it got worse. Crops from the farm weren't bringing in as much profit as Papa had hoped, and everything cost more – coffee and tea, fabric for their clothing, even the books which were Papa's one extravagance. Too, there was always the expense of poor George's upkeep.

Mama and Papa devised a plan.

Cassy and Jenny would go to school, in the house of Mrs. Cawley, a relative who lived in Oxford. Cousin Jane, only a year older than Cassy, would be there too; how cozy! Meanwhile, two new boys, paying students, would come to Papa's school and stay in the girls' room. This would ease some of the family's money worries. It would all work out beautifully, said Mama.

As she had when she was little, Jenny was to leave home. Would they be allowed to *visit,*

like James, or were they to be put aside *forever,* like George? Cassy kindly told her not to worry, that it was only for a while.

But Cassy had been wrong before.

School

*O*xford was dirty and noisy and crowded with strangers. And Mrs. Cawley was cold; she spoke to the girls as if from high atop a mountain. There were sums and reading and penmanship; there was *no* running about, *no* romping, *no* jokes that made you burst out laughing. Young ladies, Mrs. Cawley told them, sat quietly and spoke in soft voices.

You had no freedom.

Jenny missed home so badly it was like something had broken inside her.

And then Mrs. Cawley took them from *her* home to another, for Oxford, she complained, was too expensive. The little school moved to Southampton, which was cheaper, but it was also dirtier and noisier and it stank horribly of fish. Even worse, a terrible sickness swept through the town, and all three girls fell ill. Cassy and Jane felt dreadful, but Jenny was *really* sick, and not getting better.

In a daze of fever and pain, Jenny thought to herself that if her life was like a story in a book, it might end up a rather short book, with a sad ending. Why did Mrs. Cawley say they must not write to their parents? And why did she not write to them herself?

Endings

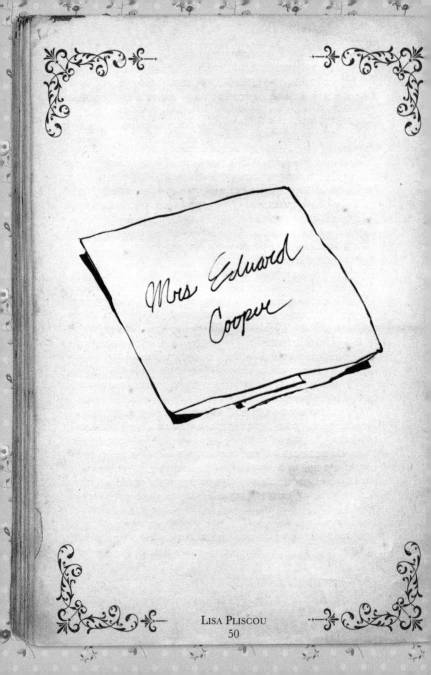

Mrs Edward
Cooper

ousin Jane – like a heroine in a novel not yet written, daring and brave and clever – managed to send a letter to her mother. As quick as Aunt Cooper could, she came, and so did Mama, only to find Jenny on the brink of death.

Fierce, determined, Mama brought Jenny back to life, and whisked her and Cassy back home.

Cousin Jane got better, too. But Aunt Cooper caught the sickness, and she died from it.

How terrible, how wrong it was! thought Jenny. Aunt Cooper should have gotten better. Cousin Jane should have been *rewarded* for her bravery. It was the wrong ending to the Southampton story.

Books

When she was finally well again, Jenny ran
and tumbled about as she used to. But
reading pulled at her, called to her. She knew
so many words now! Hundreds! Thousands!
Papa told her she might read anything in his
study. She chose a book about a man named
Sir Charles Grandison. It was an exciting love
story, seven volumes long, with a noble hero
who always said and did the right thing. She
was determined to read it from start to finish.

Two great events occurred as Jenny slowly
made her way through the volumes.

Edward left home, forever. Their cousins
Mr. and Mrs. Knight, who had no children of
their own, adopted him; he was to be their son
in the eyes of the law, and they were to raise
him up to be a great gentleman, who would
one day own their beautiful house, Godmersham, and all the land that went with it.
Edward, lucky Edward, would be *wealthy*.

A new family arrived in the neighborhood, the Lefroys. Madam Lefroy dazzled them all: she was charming and clever and kind and sweet-natured. She loved poetry and even wrote it. To Jenny's surprise and delight, there was a bright spark of understanding between herself and Madam Lefroy. And though many years separated them in age — Jenny was only eight — they became fast friends. Madam Lefroy asked questions, deep and thoughtful questions, and she listened. She heard whatever you wanted to say, no matter how whimsical or absurd. She told Jenny she could have the run of *their* library, too.

Jenny felt rich in books.

The
Abbey School

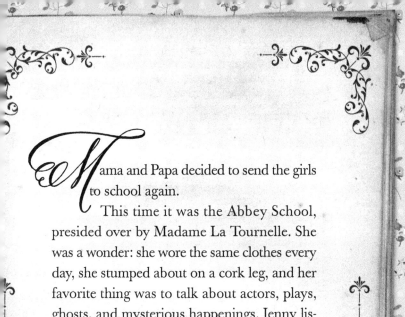

*M*ama and Papa decided to send the girls to school again.

This time it was the Abbey School, presided over by Madame La Tournelle. She was a wonder: she wore the same clothes every day, she stumped about on a cork leg, and her favorite thing was to talk about actors, plays, ghosts, and mysterious happenings. Jenny listened with wide eyes, and tried hard not to stare at her leg – although it was impossible not to make up explanations for how she had lost her real one. Jenny's favorite was the one in which Madame had formerly been a bold pirate who was worsted in a desperate scuffle over a chest of gold coins. Cassy laughed, but reminded her to keep her stories to herself.

At the Abbey School, you were taught *accomplishments* suitable for a modern young lady: spelling, penmanship, and drawing, of course, as well as needlework, music, French, and

dancing. But not a great deal of any of these, for Madame thought that a morning of education was enough. In the afternoon the girls were free to amuse themselves as they liked, to chatter and giggle and wander about the garden.

But Jenny was quiet and shy; she watched and listened, and occasionally she made a funny, pointed comment. Many of the other girls thought little Miss Jane Austen rather odd.

Cousin Eliza

*I*t seemed to Jenny that leaving the Abbey School was a Christmas gift in itself, but there was another delight in store. Cousin Eliza came to visit.

Though Eliza's letters had been for years read aloud and marveled over, Jenny had never met her. Indeed, she had never met such a person in her life. Cousin Eliza had been born in far-off India, had been given as a child a vast amount of money by her famous godfather, had traveled all over Europe. In France, she attended balls where she saw the King and Queen (and could describe, in fascinating detail, some of Marie Antoinette's amazing gowns and hairstyles); she was married to a handsome, dashing count who owned a great estate in France. How romantic! And Eliza knew all about fashion and theatre and the latest dances. Why, in London she was friendly with duchesses, and was invited to the *best*

parties, to which she traveled in her very own coach.

Lovely, laughing, affectionate Cousin Eliza fluttered about the house like some exotic bird – her dark eyes sparkling, charming them with her skill on the pianoforte, organizing little dances, interested in everyone and everything. To Jenny it seemed as if Eliza had stepped straight from the pages of a book.

The Dressing Room

*L*ike leaves in the wind, her brothers were scattering far and away, off into the wide world.

James was traveling in France, Spain, and the Netherlands. Edward was touring Sweden, Italy, and Germany (his letters pleased Mama so much that she said *he* was the writer of the family). Frank was at naval school in Portsmouth, for he was to be a sailor when he grew up.

Only little Charles was still at home, waiting his turn to follow Frank in Portsmouth, and Henry, who was going to the college in Oxford next year, and doing so well in his studies that Papa said he was the most talented of all the Austen children.

Cassy, too, was often away on long visits to relatives. Jenny missed her dreadfully, but at least she could write to her. Paper was expensive, but Papa was generous.

There were losses and there were gains.

Papa no longer took in students and the house was emptier, quieter. Cassy and Jenny were given for their very own the room adjoining theirs. They called it the Dressing Room, but it was much, much more than that.

When Cassy was home, it was a place to share stories, jokes, secrets.

When Cassy was away, Jenny could be alone.

Alone, but not lonely, for here you could think. Feel. Read. Figure things out. Dream.

Reading

*A*ll that year, with all that change, Jenny read everything she could get her hands on, dipping deep into both the library at home and at Madam Lefroy's. Poetry, plays, novels. Sermons. Essays about manners, society, life. Books about history and books about travel. It was the novels that she loved best — stories about people.

But she was reading . . . differently. Something had changed inside *herself*. She began writing little notes in the margins of books — little comments — when she found something that seemed silly or misguided. She couldn't help herself; the wrongs cried out for a response.

Like the history book that favored the awful old Queen Elizabeth over poor Mary Stuart. *No,* she wrote firmly. *No. A Lie.* And *Another Lie.*

Or Sir Charles Grandison. She used to think him a thrilling hero. Now his perfection

seemed false. Foolish. Now the noble Sir Charles made her laugh.

Or the novels whose heroines, so delicate and proper, continually wept and fainted, and were rewarded in the end for their saintly goodness. Hilarious!

As for those books that told you what to do, like *The Young Ladies Instructor*, she didn't know whether to laugh or to lose her temper. *Don't* slouch, *don't* show your ankles, *don't* blow on your soup, *don't* bite your nails, *don't* pick your nose. *Don't* talk in a loud voice. *Don't* ask a lot of questions. *Don't* have your own opinions.

Don't, don't, don't.

What *could* a girl do?

Something New

$\mathcal{C}$assy was nearly grown up. In a few years, when she too was fifteen, Jenny would be thinking of dresses and gloves, slippers and ribbons, parties and balls. Perhaps love, but certainly marriage, for that was a girl's fate. Only think of Mama, Madam Lefroy, nasty Mrs. Cawley, poor Aunt Cooper, even dashing Cousin Eliza. Marriage, a home of her own, babies.

But all that lay ahead of her — in the faraway future.

Right now, there was so much she wanted to do.

All this time she had been reading other people's words, stories, ideas. What about *hers?*

Like Mama ripping apart an old gown of Cassy's, only to put it together in a different way, creating a new gown for Jenny, Jenny was going to rip apart everything she had read. She was going to create something new, something

YOUNG JANE AUSTEN

wonderful, something wild, something funny – to make you laugh and to make you think.

She would take her place in the family circle and read *her* work out loud.

After all, it was not a *law* that there could only be one writer in a family.

Beginnings

*E*ven if you were only a girl, words made you *mighty*.

Words, stories, books: they could take you anywhere, and they could go out anywhere into the world.

Jenny – Jane – picked up her pen, and began to write.

Young Jane Austen

ANNOTATED VERSION

A Note to the Reader

If you're not familiar with Jane Austen's work, it may be helpful for you to know that she is best-known for these books, all of them novels which were published in the early 1800s:

Sense and Sensibility
Pride and Prejudice
Mansfield Park
Emma
Northanger Abbey
Persuasion

JENNY

Her story began long ago, in 1775, in a tiny village in England.

After weeks of gray fog and chilly rain, a day came that was, at last, brightened by the sun. On this day, to the Austen family was born a little girl, Jane. Everyone called her Jenny.

Slow months of bitter cold and heavy snows followed. But Jenny was warm and snug upstairs, sometimes held close to Mrs. Austen in her big soft bed, sometimes sleeping in a cozy cradle. The family tiptoed in and out, grateful that Mrs. Austen came safely through the birth, thankful for a baby that was healthy and strong.

{Notes}

16 December 1775: It is deep winter in the village of Steventon, located in the southerly rural county of Hampshire. Says Claire Tomalin in *Jane Austen: A Life,* "There were not more than thirty families living in Steventon, the single row of cottages at some distance . . . [T]here was neither shop nor inn."

What was the intellectual caliber of that remote area? According to the *Memoir of Jane Austen,* written by her nephew many years after her death, one of the neighbors went to Jane's father and asked, quite seriously, "Do tell us. Is Paris in France, or France in Paris? for my wife has been disputing with me about it."

In *Pride and Prejudice,* Mr. Darcy says, disparagingly, "In a country neighborhood you move in a very confined and un-varying society," to which Mrs. Bennet tartly retorts: "I know we dine with four and twenty families" – much to the derision of the cosmopolitan Miss Bingley.

As an adult writer, Jane Austen would remark that she specialized in "pictures of domestic Life in Country Villages" – each of her books was, she wrote with a self-deprecation which may or may not have been sincere, a "little bit (two Inches wide) of Ivory on which I work with so fine a Brush, as produces little effect after much labour."

"grateful . . . thankful": Birth was a dangerous experience for both mothers and babies. One or two women out of a hundred would die, as Roy and Leslie Adkins note in *Jane Austen's England,* and "child mortality was high."

"Jenny": While nicknames for children were just as popular as they are now, it "was rare," say the Adkins, "to give babies more than one name, and so Jane Austen and most of her con-temporaries had no middle name."

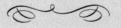

IN THE VILLAGE

Winter let go its fierce hold; icy snowdrifts melted into floods that turned the rough roads into a sea of slippery mud. Jenny was taken to Nanny Littleworth's cottage in the village. Like the other Austen babies, here she was to live until she reached what Mrs. Austen called the *age of reason* — when she could walk and say a few words and do some simple things for herself.

How strange to leave the big house where she had been born! But Nanny kept little Jenny safe and clean and dry. People came and went. As the months went by, they became familiar to her.

The tall man with the smiling eyes — that was *Papa*. And the short, slender lady who came bustling in to hug her, exclaim over her, then swiftly disappear — that was *Mama*. And five great big boys: Jemmy, George, Henry, Neddy, Frank. These were her brothers. And best of all, a girl-child, a sister — Cassy.

Jenny realized that although she lived *among* the Littleworths, she was not *of* them.

{Notes}

April 1776: Jane is four months old. "Mrs. Austen's system of childrearing was an unusual one," observes Claire Tomalin, "and was, perhaps, the practice of a busy, organized, pragmatic mother of a large family. The idea that this was an exile or an abandonment would not have occurred to Mrs. Austen; bonding between mother and child is a largely modern concept, and babies were handed about freely. It does not mean they did not suffer, both in going and in coming back."

Yet in *A Goodly Heritage,* Austen biographer George Herbert Tucker says, cursorily, that this childrearing practice was "the custom of the time," and Jane Aiken Hodge, in *Only a Novel: The Double Life of Jane Austen,* comments approvingly, "As a system, it seems to have worked admirably."

It's impossible to know whether Mrs. Austen "farmed out" her babies because it was the practice of her aristocratic relatives and she was determined to maintain this tradition, or whether she did it simply because it made her exceedingly busy life easier. Perhaps it was for both of these reasons, or for others that we can't even guess at. As for the impact on the children, that too is entirely a matter for conjecture.

HOME

One day, Jenny was taken back to the big house. Mama had told Cassy that she was to be a little mother to Jenny, so Cassy took her by the hand and showed her everything: the bedroom the two girls would share, Papa's study, the dining parlor where they ate, the sitting room, the kitchen where they mustn't bother Cook, and more. *This is home,* Cassy told her. *This is where you'll stay forever.*

It was all very different from Nanny's cottage. So many people, so many rooms! Loud, laughing boys thundering up and down the stairs, Papa coming and going, Mama seeming to be everywhere at once. The house was filled from morning till night with talking, footsteps, laughter. Noises. Words. Always words.

Jenny clung tightly to her big, kind sister.

{*Notes*}

1777: Jane is approximately eighteen months old; Cassandra is around five years old. Their close bond was one which would endure for Jane's whole life.

"the big house": The Austens lived in, but did not own, a large, rambling house with, Park Honan writes in *Jane Austen: Her Life*, "a cellar that regularly flooded and a patchwork of cracked and exposed rafters." Downstairs were two parlors or sitting rooms, Mr. Austen's study, and a kitchen; upstairs were ten bedrooms, three of which were in the attic. There was no running water, no indoor toilet, and only fireplaces with which to warm the rooms — not that the Austens would have expected anything different.

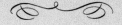

PATTERNS

Day by day, Jenny came to know the shape, the pattern, of her new life.

In the morning, there was breakfast. At the big table were Papa and Mama and Jemmy and Henry and Neddy and some other boys who *weren't* her brothers. They were Papa's students who lived here, too. Jenny's place was at a little table with Cassy and Frank.

After, she would help Cassy, as best she could, with chores. Sometimes Mama sat with Cassy and Frank and taught them letters and numbers. But not for very long, for Mama was busy. She was in charge of the housekeeping: the cooking, the cleaning, the laundry, the sewing. She told the servants what to do. And she was in charge of the vegetable garden, the fruit orchard, the poultry yard, the beehives, and the dairy, too. Baking and brewing, churning and weeding, plucking and picking, feeding and mending – there was always so much to do.

Meanwhile, Papa taught the boys in his study, and he also oversaw the family's farm, which lay up the hill just beyond the village. He rode his horse there every day, to see the crops and the animals and to talk with the people who worked for him. How very tall he looked in the saddle!

The family gathered again for dinner, and afterwards Papa would read to his students: it might be a story about strong heroes and strange monsters, or about a poor sailor shipwrecked on a faraway island, or about a brave boy who pulled a sword from a stone and learned he was to be king.

Always it was *boys* who were clever and strong and brave.

{Notes}

In 1777, Jane's siblings were James (called Jemmy), twelve years old; George, age eleven; Edward (nicknamed Neddy), ten; Henry, six years old; Cassandra (called Cassy), five; and Francis (called Frank), age four.

According to some of Austen's biographers, George, the disabled child, was boarded nearby with a village family, possibly the Littleworths, and may have, during this time, been included in some – or many – of the Austen family's activities. No one knows. Almost no information has been passed down about this "defective" child.

"Papa's students": As did many former Oxford scholars, Mr. Austen took in boarders – young male students of good birth – to supplement his income. There were likely four students at this time, ranging between five and fourteen years old. They joined the family at meals, and it's easy to imagine the clatter of silverware, the animated discussions, banter, and laughter – and a lot of dishes after to be washed.

"chores": The girls' tasks would include making their beds, clearing the tables, helping out in the garden. Mrs. Austen would be teaching Cassandra how to sew.

"servants": The Austens employed two or three maids and a manservant/gardener, as well as paying for the services of a washerwoman. (This might seem luxurious to most of us, but at that time, the Austens in their "poverty" were "reduced," says Jane Aiken Hodge, to these few servants.) Even in an era with different standards of personal cleanliness — bathing was infrequent and deodorants nonexistent — in a household of some fifteen people there had to be a good deal of laundry piling up. Claire Tomalin, in *Jane Austen: A Life*, presents a wonderfully vivid image in mentioning the washerwoman who "came once a month to tackle the piles of dirty linen, disrupting everything with steam and suds."

"Sometimes Mama sat with Cassy and Frank": Jane watches, absorbing, while her older siblings learn their letters and numbers. Mrs. Austen probably used counters and what are now called flashcards.

"dinner": The main meal of the day, taking place around three in the afternoon.

"Papa would read to his students": Mr. Austen's sons were his students too. His choice of reading would likely have included Greek mythology, *Robinson Crusoe,* the Arthurian legends. Would Jane have been eagerly listening? Mr. Austen was a kind, loving parent and it seems doubtful that he would have objected to her presence.

Play

After, there was time for play. Outside was best, if the weather would let you. You could roll down the hill at the back of the garden. You could get your fingers wet in the pond. You could join a wild game of cricket or blind man's bluff. You could run along the lane, and see the pigs at the farm. You could go to the big barn and pretend you were a king or a monster or a sailor on a tossing ship, and be as loud as you liked – even if you were a girl.

{Notes}

Biographers delight in linking youthful Jane Austen to the active, tomboyish little Catherine Morland in *Northanger Abbey.* Carol Shields evokes a halcyon childhood for Jane: "years of lightly supervised freedom, years of being 'noisy and wild,' of playing with balls instead of dolls, of rainy days spent in the barn."

There's every reason to believe that Jane – like her energetic heroine Elizabeth Bennet in *Pride and Prejudice,* who walks briskly to visit her sick sister, "jumping over stiles and springing over puddles with impatient activity, and finding herself at last within view of the house, with weary ankles, dirty stockings, and a face glowing with the warmth of exercise" – remained active as she grew up. She was "an avid walker," says Kirstin Olsen in *All Things Austen.* Since walking was the only form of exercise available to Jane as a genteel woman with a small income — horseback riding would have been out of her reach — perhaps that's why.

Or could her walks have been an essential part of her creative process, and a deliberately cultivated routine? In a report published in the *Journal of Experimental Psychology: Learning, Memory, and Cognition,* two Stanford University researchers comment, "People have noted that walking seems to have a special relation to creativity. The philosopher Friedrich Nietzsche (1889) wrote, 'All truly great thoughts are conceived by walking' (Aphorism 34). The current research puts such observations on solid footing." Researchers with a sense of humor! Their recent work has demonstrated that "walking increases creative ideation . . . and the effect even extends to when people sit down to do their creative work shortly after." Not that legions of writers — including such luminaries as Henry David Thoreau, Walt Whitman, Charles Dickens, J.K. Rowling, Virginia Woolf, Stephen King, Gretel Ehrlich, William Wordsworth, Maira Kalman, and Joyce Carol Oates — necessarily require (or would have required) the validation of scientists to prove what they already intuitively know.

"even if you were a girl": For more about the context of this phrase, see page 144.

EVENING

As the day wound down, the family came together again, this time in the sitting room. Candles were lit, Mama took up her sewing, and Papa read out loud. Sometimes it was more stories. Sometimes it was the Bible. Or the newspaper, with reports of England, India, the troubled Colonies across the great ocean. Papa might read poetry, or plays. Sometimes it was letters from relatives all over the country, or even further away: from Germany, France, the West Indies, distant, mysterious places.

But Papa wasn't the only one whose voice was heard. Mama would often comment in her quick, clever way. The boys joined in, trying to outdo each other in wit and brilliance. Jokes, ideas, laughter flew back and forth. The Austens loved to make fun of *everything*.

Then the day was over. It was a happy, drowsy time with Cassy: prayers said out loud, secrets shared, quiet giggles, and, at last, sleep.

{Notes}

"Mama would often comment": Mrs. Austen was well-known for her sharp, practical, quick-witted way of speaking, a "gift for crisp epigrammatic phrase," as David Cecil says in *A Portrait of Jane Austen,* and for her freely expressed opinions of the neighbors, irresistibly bringing to mind Mr. Bennet's wry quip in *Pride and Prejudice*: "For what do we live, but to make sport for our neighbours, and laugh at them in our turn?" Jane herself would write to Cassandra in 1799, "Whenever I fall into misfortune, how many jokes it ought to furnish to my acquaintance."

"The Austens loved to make fun of *everything*": Mr. and Mrs. Austen were proud of their intellectual and satirical outlook, fostering in their home life an environment in which the Austens — to paraphrase Elizabeth Bennet in *Pride and Prejudice* — dearly loved to laugh.

Preeminent psychologist and professor Mihaly Csikszentmihalyi in his book *Creativity: Flow and the Psychology of Discovery and Invention* maintains that creativity requires a certain context in which to best develop: "A person . . . needs *access to a domain*. This depends to a great extent on luck. Being born to an affluent family, or close to good schools, mentors, and coaches obviously is a great advantage. It does no good to be extremely intelligent and curious if I cannot learn what it takes to operate in a given symbolic system."

In Jane Austen's situation, the dominant "symbolic system," or domain, in her home was about language and literacy. She had access to neither wealth nor much formal education, but she did have the good fortune to be a member of a family that was intelligent, verbal, and lively. Csikszentmihalyi continues: "The ownership of what sociologist Pierre Bourdieu calls 'cultural capital' is a great resource. Those who have it provide their children with the advantage of an environment full of interesting books, stimulating conversation, expectations for educational advancement, role models, tutors, useful connections, and so on."

As noted elsewhere, "cultural capital" in the Austen family was shared among all the children, although it was not dispersed equally among the boys and the girls — a standard scenario of the time.

SUNDAY

Sunday was a special day, different from all the rest. In the morning and in the afternoon, the family walked up the steep hill to the gray stone church, where Papa would stand in the front and talk. For not only was Papa a teacher and a farmer, he was also the rector, helping everyone learn about God and to be better.

You had to sit very still and be very quiet and listen hard.

Jenny hardly knew what Papa was saying – she heard words like *sacrifice, resurrection, salvation; zeal, wrath, righteousness; meek, blessed, compassion* – but the syllables rolled off his tongue almost like a poem, solemn and important, that was wonderful to hear. Still, sometimes her feet got very cold.

{*Notes*}

Mr. Austen dressed in a somber black gown. The church is a small gray stone building that dated back to medieval times. One wonders if, true to the stereotype, various parishioners would be sleeping through the sermon.

It's thought by some of Jane's biographers that from earliest childhood, she unconsciously absorbed the majestic rhythms of formal speech – which she later put to good use in prose that is often so beautifully cadenced. (Incidentally, Margaret Anne Doody, in *The Jane Austen Companion,* comments that

Austen displays in her work a certain skepticism as to the power of religious tracts to alter a person's nature for the better.)

There are memorable clergymen in most of Jane Austen's novels: straitlaced Edmund Bertram in *Mansfield Park*; witty Henry Tilney in *Northanger Abbey*; the amusingly puffed-up Mr. Elton in *Emma*; diffident Edward Ferrars in *Sense and Sensibility*; and pompous Mr. Collins in *Pride and Prejudice*.

Jane's oldest brother James was ordained in 1789, when she was thirteen. According to more than one biographer, James was her least favorite brother. Other biographers, however, pass along sentimental family lore that James actively directed the young Jane's choice of reading. It's tempting to speculate that he recommended Fordyce's sententious *Sermons to Young Women* (which makes a funny appearance in *Pride and Prejudice*) once too often, and ended up, in altered form, as Mr. Collins.

WORDS DANCING

The days came and went. The seasons ebbed and flowed, each with its own pleasures and hardships, and twice each year Papa's students arrived and left for home. Life ticked on as steady as a clock. You knew what to expect, every day, every month, and you knew what was expected of you. Mama made sure of that.

But change, like a stone you tossed into the pond, rippled the smooth surface of things.

You got bigger and taller and could do more.

Jenny could dress herself – mostly. She was getting better at helping Cassy and Mama with chores. She was learning how to sew. And she had a book of her very own, which she looked at every day; it was easier than the books in Papa's study. It was about a girl who, though poor, was very good, and had many adventures and in the end was rewarded for her goodness and was married.

Jenny studied the pictures. She knew all the letters and could read *many* of the words by all herself. She whispered them out loud, just to hear the sounds they made. *Dog. Cow. Good. Poor. Pudding. Basket. Happy. Pretty.* Words danced inside her head.

{*Notes*}

"The seasons ebbed and flowed": Jane is four to six years old in this passage.

"she had a book of her very own": This was evidently one of the few children's books of the time considered a classic, *The History of Little Goody Two-Shoes*. It was a kind of extended Cinderella story which taught reading skills as well as instructing children in morals and proper behavior.

"the books in Papa's study": Mr. Austen had over 500 books in a variety of genres, an extraordinary quantity as well as a significant expense given the family's ongoing money troubles; clearly, books were a priority.

In "Secrets of the Creative Brain," a lengthy article appearing in *The Atlantic*, neuroscientist Nancy C. Andreasen describes the work of Stanford University psychologist Lewis M. Terman, who found that gifted children tended to have many books available to them at home, "with a mean of 328," says Andreasen. This number emerged from twentieth-century research, which makes the Austens' library even more impressive during a time when books were costly. And, being country folk, they lacked ready access to bookshops.

What actively fuels the development of the high-level creative mind? Mihaly Csikszentmihalyi believes that a "genetic predisposition" is likely a key aspect. He adds: "Clearly, it helps to be born in a family where intellectual behavior is practiced, or in a family that values education as an avenue of mobility – but not in a family that is comfortably middle-class." This in fact is a spot-on description of the Austen household.

"Dog. Cow. Good. Poor. Pudding. Basket. Happy. Pretty": All words from the text of *The History of Little Goody Two-Shoes*.

"Words danced": Seems like the right verb here given Jane Austen's well-known fondness for dancing from an early age — especially since the country dances of her time involved patterns and connections, which correlates to how a young writer-to-be might be making all kinds of *verbal* patterns and connections.

Indeed, Nancy C. Andreasen, who utilizes PET scanning and other sophisticated imaging techniques in her search to understand the links between the physiology of the brain and the creative process, writes that "One difference between a great writer like Shakespeare and, say, the typical stockbroker is the size and richness of the verbal lexicon in his or her temporal association cortices, as well as the complexity of the cortices' connections with other association regions in the frontal and parietal lobes."

She knows this because modern "neuroimaging tools show brain structure with a precision approximating that of the examination of post-mortem tissue; this allows researches to study all sorts of connections between brain measurements and personal characteristics."

She goes on: "For years, I had been asking myself what might be special or unique about the brains of the . . . writers I had studied. In my own version of a eureka moment, the answer finally came to me: creative people are better at recognizing relationships, making associations, and seeing things in an original way — seeing things that others cannot see."

CHANGES

The family was changing, too.

A new baby, Charles, was born. Now Jenny could be a little mother along with Cassy, running to Nanny's to hold him and play with him.

Jemmy – who wanted to be called James now – left for a faraway city called Oxford, where he was to learn many things at the college and become a great scholar and a rector, like Papa.

Neddy – Edward – went on a long journey, traveling with their cousins Mr. and Mrs. Knight.

And George, who had fits, who could neither speak nor hear, would never, Mama said, reach the age of reason, and so he was sent to live with a kind family who would take care of him, in a village far away. Mama said they must be *rational* and they must *accept*.

But Jenny puzzled over this.

Cassy – usually so wise and knowing – had been wrong. Home was *not* a place where you stayed forever: although James would come back, for visits, and Edward would return from the Knights, George had been put somewhere else. They might see him sometimes, but he would never come home.

Poor George.

Yet life went on, steady as a drumbeat. Duties and chores, games and romps, secrets with Cassy and Charles' first steps, letters coming and letters going, words and books, Papa reading and Mama sewing.

{*Notes*}

In the summer of 1779, Charles is born, the last of the eight Austen children. Two weeks later, James, age fourteen, goes to St. John's College in Oxford on a scholarship.

Edward is eleven, George thirteen.

"so he was sent to live with a kind family": Mrs. Austen's own younger brother, Tom, had been permanently put away in the care of this family, the Culhams, who lived eight miles away – a significant distance from the Austen home. It's to be hoped that they were kind. Incidentally, according to biographer Paula Bryne the extended family of Mrs. Austen was notable for "a spectacular history of madness."

Nancy C. Andreasen's neuroscience research is focused on documenting the interrelationship among creativity, genetics, and mental illness.

Creativity, she says, "tends to run in families, and to take diverse forms. In this arena, nurture clearly plays a strong role." Of the writers she's studied in the famed Iowa Writers Workshop, she notes that the "majority grew up in an environment where learning and education were highly valued."

As for mental illness, it's long been known to sometimes be closely aligned with creativity. "This link," Andreasen writes, "is not surprising. The archetype of the mad genius dates back to at least classical times, when Aristotle noted, 'Those who have been eminent in philosophy, politics, poetry, and the arts have all had tendencies toward melancholia.' This pattern is a recurring theme in Shakespeare's plays, such as when Theseus, in *A Midsummer Night's Dream,* observes, 'The lunatic, the lover, and the poet / Are of imagination all compact.' John Dryden made a similar point in a heroic couplet: 'Great wits are sure to madness near allied, / And thin partitions do their bounds divide.'"

Mihaly Csikszentmihalyi proffers a very different viewpoint in his book *Creativity: Flow and the Psychology of Discovery and Invention.* After thirty years of research, he says, "I have come to the conclusion that the reigning stereotype of the tortured genius is to large extent a myth created by Romantic ideology and supported by evidence from isolated and – one hopes – atypical historical periods."

Where does all this leave us regarding Jane Austen and mental illness? Setting aside her brother George's problems – which seem to have been more in the realm of physical handicaps – the other seven Austen children, Jane included, appear to have led reasonably balanced and productive lives. With so little concrete evidence, therefore, it would be misguided to make any assumptions in this regard.

Young Jane Austen
↪ Annotations

THE WRITER OF THE FAMILY

Christmas was always a delightful time, but this year brought a fascinating new delight. James was home, and announced that he and his brothers and their friends were going to put on a play! It was a thrilling story called *Matilda*, and James even wrote a new beginning and ending for it.

How exciting to watch the rehearsals, lively with laughter and squabbles. And what fun to finally sit in the dining parlor and see the actors, splendid in their costumes, saying their lines so well – and to be spellbound by the tale of murder and swordfights, trickery and true love, as it unfolded before your eyes!

Everyone told James how much they liked what he had written and made a great fuss over him, and about the essays and poems he had been composing, too, which he had been reading aloud to the family in the evenings. Mama declared that he was the writer of the family. It was as if, Jenny thought, he had pulled a sword from a stone. Or, rather, a pen from a stone.

And could there be only *one* writer in a family?

Mama wrote letters – many letters – and also very funny, clever verses.

Papa wrote letters as well, and the sermons which he gave on Sunday.

Weren't they writers too?

It was something else to puzzle over.

{*Notes*}

The narrative has moved from summer 1779 to December 1782. In *Jane Austen: A Life,* Claire Tomalin offers a glimpse into how Jane might have experienced the seasons: "In June there was haymaking, when the children were supplied with small hayrakes; in July there was boiling of jams and jellies; in August the harvest; in September you heard shooting. The freedom conferred by good summer weather and long hours of daylight was precious; as the year moved round and candles were lit earlier and earlier, and fires in the parlour and the dining room, the children longed for bright, frosty days that allowed them to get out of the house freely. James Austen wrote of the 'female foot' not getting through the lanes in mud, snow and flood, when men and boys could almost always manage on horseback; it was one of the sexual distinctions everyone accepted, and made bad weather a sort of imprisonment for women and girls. Itching chilblains on fingers and toes afflicted almost everyone; and Mrs. Austen caught colds that were worse than anyone else's."

"brought a fascinating new delight": In winter 1782, when Jane turned seven, the first known play at the Austens' was staged. Enthusiasm for home theatricals had been sweeping the nation for some time. Over the next few years, other, equally ambitious theatricals were staged at the Austens' home, although it's not known if Jane ever took a speaking part.

However, it seems clear that they had a significant impact on her, most notably five years later during the '87 Christmas theatricals when glamorous Cousin Eliza (see page 121) returned for a second visit and, evidently, flirted wildly with Jane's older brothers James and Henry. (Ten years later, in '97, the widowed Eliza would marry tall, handsome Henry, then twenty-five.) It seems likely that in 1787, perceptive twelve-year-old Jane would be aware of the undercurrents swirling through the house; we see them vividly articulated in the *Mansfield Park* theatricals.

"the writer of the family": As a clever six-year-old, Mrs. Austen's verses had earned her scholarly uncle's accolade as "the poet of the family."

As for James, Patrice Hannon in *101 Things You Didn't Know about Jane Austen* remarks that he was Mrs. Austen's favorite child; other biographers confirm that when Jane was a child, James was indeed considered to be the writer of the family. And according to Carol Shields, even Cassandra — Jane's beloved older sister and closest confidante, believed to be her first reader — thought of James in this light.

Leaving Home

There was never enough money, it seemed, and in the spring it got worse. Crops from the farm weren't bringing in as much profit as Papa had hoped, and everything cost more – coffee and tea, fabric for their clothing, even the books which were Papa's one extravagance. Too, there was always the expense of poor George's upkeep.

Mama and Papa devised a plan.

Cassy and Jenny would go to school, in the house of Mrs. Cawley, a relative who lived in Oxford. Cousin Jane, only a year older than Cassy, would be there too; how cozy! Meanwhile, two new boys, paying students, would come to Papa's school and stay in the girls' room. This would ease some of the family's money worries. It would all work out beautifully, said Mama.

As she had when she was little, Jenny was to leave home. Would they be allowed to *visit*, like James, or were they to be put aside *forever*, like George? Cassy kindly told her not to worry, that it was only for a while.

But Cassy had been wrong before.

{*Notes*}

Spring 1783: Jane is seven years old. Cassandra is ten, Cousin Jane Cooper eleven.

"everything cost more": The farm kept them fairly self-sufficient in terms of food supplies, but there were some household items that had to be purchased, and other expenses, of course. Prices were rising all across England, and year after year the Austens faced "the shadow of hard poverty," as Park Honan describes it in *Jane Austen: Her Life*. Money is a significant issue in all of Austen's novels, most notably in *Sense and Sensibility*, *Persuasion*, and *Pride and Prejudice*.

"Cassy and Jenny would go to school": Did Mr. and Mrs. Austen worry that Jane, at seven, was too young to be sent away from home? Years later, Mrs. Austen declared that it was Jane's own decision to be sent to the Abbey School at age nine: "if Cassandra's head had been going to be cut off, Jane would have her's [sic] cut off too." Claire Tomalin in *Jane Austen: A Life*, says that if this is an accurate report, "it makes the earlier decision even harder to understand."

Mrs. Ann Cawley was the widowed sister of Mrs. Austen's brother-in-law.

The girls likely traveled the fifty miles to Oxford by stagecoach; it's not known if Mr. Austen, or James, traveled with them.

Some biographers believe that Jane's experience of being sent away from home at such a young age is reflected in the poignant episode of ten-year-old Fanny Price's uprooting from her home and difficult transition into the Bertram household in *Mansfield Park*. The word "home" appears many times throughout that work: it "is repeated over 140 times," as Paula Bryne points out.

The concept of "home" can be a key component in the traditional love story, and is very evident in Austen's work, most satisfyingly in *Pride and Prejudice* and *Persuasion,* in which her heroines ultimately occupy with their beloved husbands a new home where they are, at last, understood and valued for their true worth.

This element was a constant one in Austen's own life, as she was episodically removed from home: as an infant, twice during her schoolgirl days, and at age twenty-five when her father abruptly gave up his rectorate and took Mrs. Austen, the still unmarried Cassandra, and Jane (also unmarried) to Bath, located sixty-five miles from Steventon. They then shifted among increasingly modest rented lodgings until finally, Jane's wealthy brother Edward offered them – Mr. Austen had by this time died – the use of a cottage he owned in Chawton, in the south of England, where Jane spent the last eight years of her life. (Whenever one hears the word "cottage" in connection with Jane Austen, it likely summons up the ridiculous remark by pampered fop Robert Ferrars in *Sense and Sensibility*: "I am excessively fond of a cottage; there is always so much comfort, so much elegance to them." This he says to Elinor Dashwood, who has been forced by her sudden father's death to leave her large elegant home and live instead, thanks to the generosity of her mother's cousin, in a small cottage "with dark narrow stairs, and a kitchen that smokes," as Elinor wryly describes it.)

Reflecting on Jane's move from Steventon when she was twenty-five, Carol Shields comments mournfully: "Home was what she loved best. . . . Home also meant psychological security – daily routines, old friends, acceptance, usefulness to those she loved, and the series of small accomplishments that gave purpose to her existence." In Bath, Jane Austen evidently wrote little.

"There is nothing," Jane would later write by way of chatty Mrs. Elton in *Emma*, "like staying at home for real comfort."

SCHOOL

Oxford was dirty and noisy and crowded with strangers. And Mrs. Cawley was cold; she spoke to the girls as if from high atop a mountain. There were sums and reading and penmanship; there was *no* running about, *no* romping, *no* jokes that made you burst out laughing. Young ladies, Mrs. Cawley told them, sat quietly and spoke in soft voices.

You had no freedom.

Jenny missed home so badly it was like something had broken inside her.

And then Mrs. Cawley took them from *her* home to another, for Oxford, she complained, was too expensive. The little school moved to Southampton, which was cheaper, but it was also dirtier and noisier and it stank horribly of fish. Even worse, a terrible sickness swept through the town, and all three girls fell ill. Cassy and Jane felt dreadful, but Jenny was *really* sick, and not getting better.

In a daze of fever and pain, Jenny thought to herself that if her life was like a story in a book, it might end up a rather short book, with a sad ending. Why did Mrs. Cawley say they must not write to their parents? And why did she not write to them herself?

{*Notes*}

The girls went to Oxford in the spring of 1783; then to Southampton in September.

"it stank horribly of fish": As a teenager, Jane would turn this near-fatal experience to good account in her funny, clever little novel *Love and Freindship [sic]*, in which a worldly matron advises her young friend Marianne: "Beware of the insipid Vanities and idle Dissipation of the Metropolis of England; Beware of the unmeaning Luxuries of Bath and of the Stinking fish of Southampton."

Southampton was a bustling port town, filled with sailors and soldiers returning from abroad. The girls caught a highly contagious and often lethal illness: probably typhus, although nobody knows for sure.

"Why did Mrs. Cawley say they must not write to their parents?": For reasons unknown, Mrs. Cawley never wrote to either of the two sets of parents to alert them to their daughters' illness, and she also forbade the girls to write. Jane Cooper must have been a remarkable person to have defied Mrs. Cawley's order.

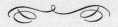

Endings

Cousin Jane – like a heroine in a novel not yet written, daring and brave and clever – managed to send a letter to her mother. As quick as Aunt Cooper could, she came, and so did Mama, only to find Jenny on the brink of death.

Fierce, determined, Mama brought Jenny back to life, and whisked her and Cassy back home.

Cousin Jane got better, too. But Aunt Cooper caught the sickness, and she died from it.

How terrible, how wrong it was! thought Jenny. Aunt Cooper should have gotten better. Cousin Jane should have been *rewarded* for her bravery. It was the wrong ending to the Southampton story.

{*Notes*}

October 1783: Aunt Cooper – Mrs. Austen's sister, Jane – dies in Bath. Jane Austen visited Bath as a girl and lived there for a time as an adult; she is generally thought to have detested it. Much of *Persuasion* takes place there: sensitive, warmhearted Anne Elliot dislikes Bath as it's where her beloved mother died.

Aunt Cooper's grieving husband, Dr. Edward Cooper, later sent the girls "small tokens," says David Nokes in *Jane Austen: A Life,* "by which to remember their courageous aunt." Cassandra received a ring, and Jane a headband which she would wear at balls when she was older.

BOOKS

When she was finally well again, Jenny ran and tumbled about as she used to. But reading pulled at her, called to her. She knew so many words now! Hundreds! Thousands! Papa told her she might read anything in his study. She chose a book about a man named Sir Charles Grandison. It was an exciting love story, seven volumes long, with a noble hero who always said and did the right thing. She was determined to read it from start to finish.

Two great events occurred as Jenny slowly made her way through the volumes.

Edward left home, forever. Their cousins Mr. and Mrs. Knight, who had no children of their own, adopted him; he was to be their son in the eyes of the law, and they were to raise him up to be a great gentleman, who would one day own their beautiful house, Godmersham, and all the land that went with it. Edward, lucky Edward, would be *wealthy*.

A new family arrived in the neighborhood, the Lefroys. Madam Lefroy dazzled them all: she was charming and clever and kind and sweet-natured. She loved poetry and even wrote it. To Jenny's surprise and delight, there was a bright spark of understanding between herself and Madam Lefroy. And though many years separated them in age – Jenny was only eight – they became fast friends. Madam Lefroy asked questions, deep and thoughtful questions, and she listened. She heard whatever you wanted to say, no matter how whimsical or absurd. She told Jenny she could have the run of *their* library, too.

Jenny felt rich in books.

{Notes}

"reading pulled at her": Claire Tomalin notes Jane's brother Henry's "remembrance of a very young and precocious child curled over her books"; he also remarked upon her "tenacious memory."

"Edward left home": He is sixteen. Austen scholars believe that Edward's adoption is reflected in the plots of *Emma* – Frank Churchill is legally adopted as the heir of wealthy childless relatives, and Jane Fairfax is informally adopted by the Campbell family – and *Mansfield Park,* in which Fanny Price is informally adopted by her affluent relatives, the Bertrams.

Godmersham was 100 miles away. In later years, Jane visited there frequently and was able to view the lives of the wealthy leisured class firsthand – and to experience it as a poor relation. This she seems to have effectively utilized in *Pride and Prejudice* and *Mansfield Park.* Both her parents were, in fact, poor relations themselves, sometimes recipients of largess, sometimes disappointed in their hopes for assistance or legacies.

"A large income," Jane would later write in the arch voice of *Mansfield Park*'s Mary Crawford, "is the best recipe for happiness I ever heard of."

Some biographers believe that Madam Lefroy was the inspiration for Anne Elliot's older friend and mentor Lady Russell in *Persuasion.* It's an especially intriguing notion when one considers Madam Lefroy's possible involvement in ending Jane's romance at age nineteen/twenty with Tom Lefroy. (More about this on page 145.)

Curiously, *Persuasion*'s Anne Elliot is nineteen when she rejects Frederick Wentworth's first offer of marriage; the novel begins when she is twenty-seven, the precise age of Jane Austen when she received, and rejected, her only known marriage proposal. Charlotte Lucas in *Pride and Prejudice* is twenty-seven when she pragmatically accepts Mr. Collins' sudden proposal following Elizabeth Bennet's decisive rejection.

THE ABBEY SCHOOL

Mama and Papa decided to send the girls to school again.

This time it was the Abbey School, presided over by Madame La Tournelle. She was a wonder: she wore the same clothes every day, she stumped about on a cork leg, and her favorite thing was to talk about actors, plays, ghosts, and mysterious happenings. Jenny listened with wide eyes, and tried hard not to stare at her leg – although it was impossible not to make up explanations for how she had lost her real one. Jenny's favorite was the one in which Madame had formerly been a bold pirate who was worsted in a desperate scuffle over a chest of gold coins. Cassy laughed, but reminded her to keep her stories to herself.

At the Abbey School, you were taught *accomplishments* suitable for a modern young lady: spelling, penmanship, and drawing, of course, as well as needlework, music, French, and dancing. But not a great deal of any of these, for Madame thought that a morning of education was enough. In the afternoon the girls were free to amuse themselves as they liked, to chatter and giggle and wander about the garden.

But Jenny was quiet and shy; she watched and listened, and occasionally she made a funny, pointed comment. Many of the other girls thought little Miss Jane Austen rather odd.

{Notes}

August 1785: Jane is nine, Cassandra twelve, Jane Cooper thirteen.

The Abbey School was in Reading, twenty miles from Steventon. This busy town was filled with mills and brewing works, and wagons traveling between London and Bath.

Mr. and Mrs. Austen may have scraped together the money to send their daughters to this larger, more well-established school than that of Mrs. Cawley for the express purpose of acquiring genteel "accomplishments" considered desirable on the marriage market.

Madame La Tournelle – actually Sarah Hackitt – was a fat, cheerful woman with a mysterious cork leg; she wasn't French, spoke no French, and had never been to France, but her assumption of the name gave the school a certain fashionable cachet. The Abbey School was next to the ruins of an old monastery: very Gothic, and how Catherine Morland in *Northanger Abbey* would have enjoyed it! In their ample free time the girls were allowed to wander in the garden that overlooked the ruins.

"it was impossible not to make up explanations for how she had lost her real one": A niece of Jane Austen would later describe her aunt's habit of "imagining . . . impossible contingencies . . . coloured to her own fancy."

The Abbey School could well have been the model for Mrs. Goddard's school in *Emma*. Both in Jane's letters and in her work, we get the impression that she heartily disliked her school experiences. In *Sense and Sensibility,* for example, the narrator makes a deeply ironic remark about Charlotte

Palmer's seven years at school; in *Emma* we hear about expensive schools in which both the physical and mental health of girls are damaged.

Park Honan in *Jane Austen: Her Life* speculates that it was here, in a setting that included girls from a higher social strata, that Jane — coming from a financially insecure family on the lower fringes of the gentry — encountered her first strong dose of class consciousness. (In the years to come, themes of class and money would dominate all her novels.) About Jane's experience at the Abbey School, Honan muses, "Ordinary life can be more horrifying than horror fiction and a girls' school consists of other girls."

"rather odd": Austen's more sensitive biographers point to letters both from Jane and about Jane which suggest that she may have been quirky, offbeat, *different* — and thought odd, as precocious children often are.

COUSIN ELIZA

It seemed to Jenny that leaving the Abbey School was a Christmas gift in itself, but there was another delight in store. Cousin Eliza came to visit.

Though Eliza's letters had been for years read aloud and marveled over, Jenny had never met her. Indeed, she had never met such a person in her life. Cousin Eliza had been born in far-off India, had been given as a child a vast amount of money by her famous godfather, had traveled all over Europe. In France, she attended balls where she saw the King and Queen (and could describe, in fascinating detail, some of Marie Antoinette's amazing gowns and hairstyles); she was married to a handsome, dashing count who owned a great estate in France. How romantic! And Eliza knew all about fashion and theatre and the latest dances. Why, in London she was friendly with duchesses, and was invited to the *best* parties, to which she traveled in her very own coach.

Lovely, laughing, affectionate Cousin Eliza fluttered about the house like some exotic bird – her dark eyes sparkling, charming them with her skill on the pianoforte, organizing little dances, interested in everyone and everything. To Jenny it seemed as if Eliza had stepped straight from the pages of a book.

{*Notes*}

December 1786: After some sixteenth months at the Abbey

School, Jane and Cassandra return home; their formal education is over. Jane turns eleven this December.

Twenty-five-year-old Cousin Eliza, the Comtesse de Feuillide, arrives with her six-month-old baby Hastings. Her husband remains in France. Eliza was slim, petite, and vivacious, a dazzling vision of beauty and glamour. It's believed that she was the model for Mary Crawford in *Mansfield Park* and, in a more favorably rendered form, Elizabeth Bennet in *Pride and Prejudice*. Some also believe she may have influenced the character of the venal, manipulative Lady Susan, the antihero of Austen's first real novel. And, of course, there is the use of her name in *Sense and Sensibility*: the tragic Eliza and her unfortunate daughter, also named Eliza, who succumbs to Willoughby's dishonorable advances.

There are further wisps of connections to *Sense and Sensibility*: before Jane Austen was born, Cousin Eliza's mother, Philadelphia, at the age of twenty-two had traveled to exotic, far-off India in search of a husband, where she had quickly met and married an English physician. The subject of India makes its appearance by way of Colonel Brandon's military experience there.

"a handsome, dashing count": The *comte* was certainly handsome and dashing, but it does seem that he was very interested in Eliza's money, as most of his estate was in urgent need of draining. Eliza, for her part, boasted of the *comte*'s devotion to her, which she accepted placidly, not displaying a great deal of affection in return. A few years later the *comte* would be guillotined in the French Revolution. There's speculation that he was an impostor who had murdered the real *comte* and taken on his identity. Romantic indeed!

As for young Jane seeing only the glamorous aspects of Eliza's fantastical marriage and lifestyle, children, of course, can have a very different take on things as compared to the more sophisticated perspective of adults. It's possible that Jane's nature was one that responded intuitively to such Cinderella-like tropes. In 1998's *Please Understand Me II: Temperament, Character, Intelligence,* author David Keirsey's description of the "Idealist" personality seems to dovetail in many ways with what we know about Austen, particularly in her affinity for books and her gifts as a wordsmith, both enthusiasms that she manifested at a young age.

"It may seem strange," Keirsey says, "to describe Idealist children as 'romantic,' but they certainly are romantic in the sense that, as they look for their unique qualities, they are apt to identify with characters in stories. When very young, [they] usually enjoy being read stories which are beyond their own reading capabilities, but which fire their imagination. Fairy tales and children's stories . . . are all real for the Idealist child to a degree not shared by other types." He goes on to say that these children love "stories that have happy endings, with heroes winning, and even villains having a change of heart in the end. Such happily-ever-after stories capture Idealist kids from the very beginning and never let go of them, however much their hopes and dreams are defied by reality."

People of this type "are naturally inductive in their thought and speech, which is to say that they move quickly from part to whole, from a few particulars to sweeping generalizations, from the smallest sign of something to its entirety" – an observation that brings to mind what is probably Austen's most famous line of writing, the epigrammatic "It is a truth universally acknowledged, that a single man in possession of a good fortune must be in want of a wife," which begins *Pride and Prejudice*.

"In all areas of life," Keirsey says, "Idealists are concerned not so much with practical realities as with meaningful possibilities, with romantic ideals . . . they want their relationships to be deep and meaningful, full of beauty, poetry, and sensitivity." He goes on: "What Idealists wish for in their spouse is a Soulmate, a spouse who knows their feelings without being told of them, and who spontaneously expresses words of endearment, words that acknowledge their mate's unique identity. Idealists want the marital relationship to be, as they put it, 'deep and meaningful.' Other types will settle for much less than this."

Perhaps this insight helps us understand why Austen rejected an offer of marriage that was eminently practical. It wasn't, apparently, tendered from a man she could truly love. Harris Bigg-Wither was said to be an unprepossessing, even boorish young man, neither intellectually inclined nor able to converse with any degree of wit or tact. If this is an accurate description, he and Jane would hardly seem to have made a compatible couple. (More about this on page 146.)

Some years later, Jane had her heroine Anne say in *Persuasion*: "My idea of good company, Mr. Elliot, is the company of clever, well-informed people, who have a great deal of conversation; that is what I call good company."

And her companion, the attractive and intelligent William Elliot, responds, "You are mistaken . . . that is not good company; that is the best."

The Dressing Room

Like leaves in the wind, her brothers were scattering far and away, off into the wide world.

James was traveling in France, Spain, and the Netherlands. Edward was touring Sweden, Italy, and Germany (his letters pleased Mama so much that she said *he* was the writer of the family). Frank was at naval school in Portsmouth, for he was to be a sailor when he grew up.

Only little Charles was still at home, waiting his turn to follow Frank in Portsmouth, and Henry, who was going to the college in Oxford next year, and doing so well in his studies that Papa said he was the most talented of all the Austen children.

Cassy, too, was often away on long visits to relatives. Jenny missed her dreadfully, but at least she could write to her. Paper was expensive, but Papa was generous.

There were losses and there were gains. Papa no longer took in students and the house was emptier, quieter. Cassy and Jenny were given for their very own the room adjoining theirs. They called it the Dressing Room, but it was much, much more than that.

When Cassy was home, it was a place to share stories, jokes, secrets.

When Cassy was away, Jenny could be alone.

Alone, but not lonely, for here you could think. Feel. Read. Figure things out. Dream.

{*Notes*}

1787: Jane is eleven. James is twenty-one, Edward twenty, Henry fifteen, Cassandra fourteen, Francis thirteen, Charles six.

"Like leaves in the wind": Anne Elliot in *Persuasion* eloquently sums up the gender divide of Jane Austen's time: "We certainly do not forget you [men], so soon as you forget us. It is, perhaps, our fate rather than our merit. We cannot help ourselves. We live at home, quiet, confined, and our feelings prey upon us. You are forced on exertion. You have always a profession, pursuits, business of some sort or other, to take you back into the world immediately . . ."

As a kind of societal consolation prize, females were permitted to *read* about male exploits. Discussing such books as the best-selling *Robinson Crusoe,* authors of the popular treatise *Practical Education* (1798) said cautiously, "To girls this species of reading cannot be as dangerous as it is to boys: girls must soon perceive the impossibility of their rambling about the world in quest of adventures."

Francis and Charles' successful careers in the navy will provide excellent material for *Persuasion* and, in a smaller way, for *Mansfield Park*.

It is unknown as to whether Cassandra and Jane were corresponding at this point (the earliest surviving letters begin when Jane is twenty), although we do know that Mr. Austen was indeed generous with paper, both for Jane's "effusions of fancy," as he once playfully called her writing, and Cassandra's artwork.

"Papa no longer took in students": Biographers don't agree on this point. Some say he still did — possibly fewer.

In the Dressing Room were such items as an armoire, a mirror, books, Jane's pianoforte, a table that held the two girls' work boxes containing their sewing supplies, and, later, Jane's tabletop writing desk, thought to be a gift from her father on her nineteenth birthday. It's possible that Cassandra, who liked to draw and paint, kept her art supplies here as well. Biographers believe that Jane's first literary efforts were written in the Dressing Room.

"think. Feel. Read. Figure things out. Dream": In an article appearing in *Scientific American,* Nessa Victoria Bryce describes how researchers studying the cognitive process of creativity have identified five distinct stages: *exploration* (during which you gather a broad base of knowledge), *focus* (you're practicing, studying, and developing skills in your area of deep interest), *incubation* (a time during which it may seem to an outsider observer that you're not making progress but are, in fact, doing so, possibly even on unconscious levels, and often while you're doing mundane tasks), *insight* (the "aha!" moment, when everything seems to come together in a new and exciting way), and *evaluation* (when you take the time to make sure your idea is a good one, and, perhaps, share your work with people you trust).

The text in "The Dressing Room" doesn't necessarily correlate exactly to the stages described here, but in looking at Jane Austen's life as a whole, her experiences and her literary output seem to align with this framework quite well.

READING

All that year, with all that change, Jenny read everything she could get her hands on, dipping deep into both the library at home and at Madam Lefroy's. Poetry, plays, novels. Sermons. Essays about manners, society, life. Books about history and books about travel. It was the novels that she loved best – stories about people.

But she was reading . . . differently. Something had changed inside *herself*. She began writing little notes in the margins of books – little comments – when she found something that seemed silly or misguided. She couldn't help herself; the wrongs cried out for a response.

Like the history book that favored the awful old Queen Elizabeth over poor Mary Stuart. *No,* she wrote firmly. *No. A Lie*. And *Another Lie*.

Or Sir Charles Grandison. She used to think him a thrilling hero. Now his perfection seemed false. Foolish. Now the noble Sir Charles made her laugh.

Or the novels whose heroines, so delicate and proper, continually wept and fainted, and were rewarded in the end for their saintly goodness. Hilarious!

As for those books that told you what to do, like *The Young Ladies Instructor*, she didn't know whether to laugh or to lose her temper. *Don't* slouch, *don't* show your ankles, *don't* blow on your soup, *don't* bite your nails, *don't* pick your nose. *Don't* talk in a loud voice. *Don't* ask a lot of questions. *Don't* have your own opinions.

Don't, don't, don't.
What *could* a girl do?

{*Notes*}

1787: Continues.

"read everything she could get her hands on": Neuroscientist Nancy C. Andreasen comments, "Many creative people are autodidacts," thriving in an environment in which they can pursue their interests at their own pace. They also "tend to be very persistent, even when confronted with skepticism or rejection." As noted in the "About Jane Austen" section on pages 139–156, perseverance played a critical role in Jane's development both as a writer and as a published author.

"It was the novels that she loved best": Jane Austen's interest in novels of all sorts, from literary to trashy, is well documented. In *Northanger Abbey* the narrator describes the novel (presumably without Jane's trademark irony) as a means by which "the greatest powers of the mind are displayed, in which the most thorough knowledge of human nature, the happiest delineation of its varieties, the liveliest effusions of wit and humor are conveyed to the world in the best chosen language."

Mihaly Csikszentmihalyi finds it useful to take a systems approach to creativity, describing how it most often flourishes in a sort of congenial sociocultural petri dish. "When we asked creative persons what explains their success, one of the most frequent answers – perhaps the most frequent one – was that they were lucky. Being in the right place at the right time is an almost universal explanation."

As it happens, Austen came of age during a time when the English publishing industry was fairly crackling with enthusiasm for the artistic and commercial potential of the novel. (More about this on page 147.)

"She began writing little notes in the margins of books": Biographer Paula Byrne comments on how Jane at this age displayed "the almost uncontainable urge to scribble that is the mark of the born writer."

In addition, at some point in her youth, Jane wrote up several imaginary marriages for herself in her father's parish register. It's fascinating to see the names "Fitzwilliam" (Mr. Darcy's first name in *Pride and Prejudice*) and "Edmund" (as in *Mansfield Park*'s love interest Edmund Bertram) show up. Her biographers conjure the appealing image of kind, indulgent Mr. Austen laughing at young Jane's literary prank.

". . . continually wept and fainted": This cult of exaggerated sensibility is a lively theme in *Northanger Abbey*. It's a theme Austen explored in a more serious way in *Sense and Sensibility*, with her portrayal of the lovely, sensitive, impulsive Marianne Dashwood.

Some Austen experts speculate that in the contrast between the two Dashwood sisters we may see hints of Jane Austen and her older sister Cassandra, with Jane more aligned with Marianne and the reserved and pragmatic Elinor (the older sister) bearing some resemblance to Cassandra.

"those books that told you what to do": Instructional manuals or "conduct books" for girls and women – what we might today call "self-help" books – were wildly popular in Britain before, during, and after Jane Austen's time. Writes Nancy Armstrong in *Desire and Domestic Fiction,* "So popular did these books become that by the second half of the eighteenth century virtually everyone knew the ideal of womanhood they proposed."

What was the ideal young lady like? She was modest, obedient, pious, sweet-natured, chaste, and self-effacing. And when she was married? "To the qualities of the innocent maiden, conduct books appended those of the efficient housewife" – she was frugal, energetic, capable, and selfless. And obedient to her husband, of course, who, quite literally, owned her.

Something New

Cassy was nearly grown up. In a few years, when she too was fifteen, Jenny would be thinking of dresses and gloves, slippers and ribbons, parties and balls. Perhaps love, but certainly marriage, for that was a girl's fate. Only think of Mama, Madam Lefroy, nasty Mrs. Cawley, poor Aunt Cooper, even dashing Cousin Eliza. Marriage, a home of her own, babies.

But all that lay ahead of her – in the faraway future.

Right now, there was so much she wanted to do.

All this time she had been reading other people's words, stories, ideas. What about *hers?*

Like Mama ripping apart an old gown of Cassy's, only to put it together in a different way, creating a new gown for Jenny, Jenny was going to rip apart everything she had read. She was going to create something new, something wonderful, something wild, something funny – to make you laugh and to make you think.

She would take her place in the family circle and read *her* work out loud.

After all, it was not a *law* that there could only be one writer in a family.

{Notes}

1787: The year Jane turns twelve. Most scholars and biographers agree that this is when, writing with focus and inventiveness, she began her literary career.

Cassandra is fifteen. At sixteen, a girl would be "out" in society and could begin going to balls, parties, and other social gatherings, thus starting on the path toward matrimony.

"Marriage, a home of her own, babies": Carol Shields suggests that Mr. and Mrs. Bennet in *Pride and Prejudice* are altered portraits of Jane Austen's parents. In Mr. Bennet – the intelligent reading man who tends to his estate's farm; is not, perhaps, very shrewd in money matters; and shares a special, warm relationship with his bright daughter Elizabeth – we may see Mr. Austen and Jane. Similarly, in Mrs. Bennet who, despite her shrillness, is quite sensible in her determination to see her poorly dowered daughters settled in life, we may catch a glimpse of Mrs. Austen, a practical lady profoundly concerned with successfully launching her numerous offspring into the world.

"Like Mama ripping apart an old gown of Cassy's": Margaret Anne Doody, in "Jane Austen's Reading" in *The Jane Austen Companion,* points out several instances in Austen's work where she utilizes bits and pieces of names, characters, phrases, and plot elements from among her wide and varied reading. In Austen's early writing as a teenager can be found names that will reappear in her mature work: Jane, Henry, Frank, Edward, Eliza, Emma, Catherine, Marianne, Frederic, Lucy, Charlotte, Fanny, Elliott, Willoughby, Crawford, Dashwood . . .

"You cannot transform a domain unless you first thoroughly understand how it works," says Mihaly Csikszentmihalyi. "Which means that one has to acquire the tools of mathematics, learn the basic principles of physics, and become aware of the current state of knowledge. But the old Italian saying seems to apply: *Impara l'arte, e mettila da parte* (learn the craft, and then set it aside). One cannot be creative without learning what others know, but then one cannot be creative without becoming dissatisfied with that knowledge and rejecting it (or some of it) for a better way."

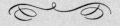

BEGINNINGS

Even if you were only a girl, words made you *mighty*.

Words, stories, books: they could take you anywhere, and they could go out anywhere into the world.

Jenny – Jane – picked up her pen, and began to write.

{*Notes*}

"picked up her pen": It would indeed be the emblematic writing instrument of that era: a goose-quill pen. An expensive item, and in constant need of mending.

"began to write": In a section called "Affinity and Persistence," renowned Harvard psychologist Howard Gardner is quoted in *The Creative Spirit* as saying, "The most important thing at the beginning is for an individual to feel some kind of emotional connection to something." Albert Einstein, for example, developed a fascination for physics when he was only five years old. Gardner believes that "childhood moments are one key to understanding creative lives. 'Without that initial love and emotional connection, I think that the chances of doing good creative work later on are minimal. . . . But the initial intoxication is not enough in itself. It essentially moves you to take steps to learn more about the thing that first interests you, and to discover its complexities, its difficulties, its strengths and obscurities.'

"From that initial love of doing something comes persistence. People who care passionately about what they are doing don't give up easily. When frustration comes, they persist. When people are resistant to their innovation, they keep going anyway. As Thomas Edison said, 'Sticking to it is the genius!'"

About Jane Austen

JANE AUSTEN went on to write six novels which have become some of the most famous, most loved books in the world. They've been translated into many languages, made into movies and TV shows, and inspired countless books, articles, websites, and blogs as well as a mind-boggling array of merchandise.

When we first learn about an author from long ago, especially someone who's now so popular as Jane Austen, it's easy to think that she or he was *always* a solidly established writer. But people aren't *born* writers; they *become* writers. They're shaped by the circumstances of their lives — their personality, their interests, their experiences, their family and friends — and it's never a certain thing that a talent with words, no matter how abundant, will find its full expression in both accomplishment and recognition.

Jane Austen faced daunting challenges in her journey toward becoming a writer.

What Was She *Like?*

THIS BOOK is an attempt to figure out how young Jane took those first key steps. Because we're pretty sure that she was around twelve years old when she first began to write in earnest, I wanted to look backward into her early life as a child.

Unfortunately, we know so little about her during this time. Even some of the basic facts of her existence are in dispute among her various biographers. Our primary sources of solid – or *somewhat* solid – information are material written by relatives long after Jane Austen had died and a small batch of her letters. These, of course, are subject to interpretation.

In describing Jane Austen to an increasingly enthusiastic public, her relatives seemed keen to create a simplistic image of Jane as a quiet, self-sacrificing, perpetually cheerful person, almost saintly in her goodness: just the sort of character in a book whom Jane would have despised – or laughed at. In fact, in a letter to her niece Fanny Knight she wrote about such idealized heroines: "Pictures of perfection, as you know, make me sick and wicked." This suggests to us a much livelier, much more *interesting* personality.

Indeed, in a discussion of the traits that distinguish creative people, Mihaly Csikszentmihalyi observes, "If I had to express in one word what makes their personalities different from others, it would be *complexity*. By this I mean that they show tendencies of thought and action that in most people are segregated. They contain contradictory extremes – instead of being an 'individual,' each of them is a 'multitude.' Like the color white that includes all the hues in the spectrum, they tend to bring together the entire range of human possibilities within themselves."

As for Jane Austen's letters, only a small portion of her vivid, funny, detailed correspondence is available to us today. Most of her recipients didn't keep her letters. Cassandra did, but a few years after Jane died, she either edited them or destroyed them.

My goal in writing this book was to portray the young Jane Austen in a way that reminds us that she actually was a real person and, like all of us, one with strengths and weaknesses, subject to the highs and lows we all go through. The events that together form the narrative's framework are those that are generally accepted as fact.

Time and Place

To TRULY understand Jane Austen's greatness, we've got to think about her in terms of *when* she lived and *where*.

She was born in England in 1775.

Some readers might think I'm being unkind to Jane by including in the text the phrases "even if you were a girl" and "only a girl," but during that time, girls and women were generally thought to be less interesting, less intelligent, even less worthwhile than boys and men. Some Austen biographers go even further by suggesting that Jane's parents, driven by the urgent need to keep the family financially afloat, were focused more on their sons, who would become wage-earners, than on their daughters who, with luck, would someday become the financial responsibility of their husbands. All of which makes Jane's accomplishments — the remarkable result of both her talent and her determination — even more impressive.

It's also important to know that during this period in history, most people had fixed ideas about a person's "class" — your place on a kind of social ladder that indicated to others how you were to be thought about, categorized, and talked to. You knew who was your "better" and you knew who was "lesser."

At the very top of the ladder, of course, were the kings and queens, and at the very bottom were the poor people. Your spot on the ladder was largely determined by who your family was, and it wasn't so easy to shift upwards on the ladder (although going *down* it was easier).

Jane Austen's brother Edward was one of the lucky few who were able to shoot up the ladder, thanks to his adoption by wealthy cousins. Mr. and Mrs. Austen occupied a rung that today we might call the middle class, but certainly not the upper rung of that group: they were *respectable*, but they didn't own land and didn't have much money.

Another important thing to realize about Jane Austen is that for a girl in her class, the *only* "career" she could aspire to was getting married. Even that wasn't a certainty, for during those days a woman who didn't bring money of her own into a marriage could have a difficult time finding a husband. An "old maid" – an unmarried woman – could easily become a financial burden to her family, and might find the shame difficult to bear.

Coming as she did from a family that had money problems, Jane Austen's marriage prospects were limited. It's believed that when she was nineteen, she fell in love with a young man, Tom Lefroy, who was visiting the area and who returned her feelings, but because neither of them had any money, his family had him sent away and in this manner ended the romance.

When she was twenty-seven — and very much in the danger zone of being an "old maid" — Jane received a proposal from a well-to-do young man she'd known for many years. By accepting Harris Bigg-Wither's offer, she could have been financially secure for the first time in her life, and made sure that her elderly parents and her unmarried sister Cassandra were secure as well. But after initially saying yes, the very next day she changed her mind.

Years later, when her niece Fanny asked for her advice on the subject of love and marriage, Jane Austen wrote in reply, "Anything is to be preferred or endured rather than marrying without Affection." It's possible that she was referring to own dilemma when faced with a difficult choice.

Yet despite writing to Fanny that "Single women have a dreadful propensity for being poor. Which is one very strong argument in favor of matrimony," Austen herself had chosen the path of poverty. But she had also, perhaps, chosen to retain her freedom: instead of transforming herself into the legal property of her husband and risking the very real dangers of childbirth, possibly many times over, she was free to continue to pursue her art.

A New and Different Type of Book

A *NOVEL* is a work of fiction — that is, it's a made-up story about imaginary people. In our time, we're completely accustomed to this type of book, but in Jane Austen's era, novels — as the word itself suggests — were something fairly new and different. For the first time, writers were trying to get into the minds of their characters, and to convincingly portray them as people you might meet in real life.

It was a momentous development, and a popular one, creating a rapidly growing audience for this type of book. Still, many people were suspicious of them, and considered them particularly dangerous for girls. In *Desire and Domestic Fiction* author Nancy Armstrong quotes from an influential British book published in 1798, *Practical Education,* which warned of the dire consequences of novel-reading: "With respect to sentimental stories, and books of mere entertainment, we must remark, that they should be sparingly used, especially in the education of girls. This species of reading cultivates what is called the heart prematurely, lowers the tone of the mind, and induces indifference for those common pleasures and occupations which, however trivial in themselves, constitute by far the greatest portion of our daily happiness."

So much for reading. What about writing? A very few women published novels, but many of them did so anonymously, as it was thought to be an unladylike activity to attempt to put yourself in the public eye. Mary Brunton, a successful British novelist of the early 1800s, remarked that she "would sooner exhibit as a rope-dancer" than be openly acknowledged as a lady who published books.

As an adult, Jane Austen would defiantly write in the voice of *Persuasion*'s Anne Elliot, "Men have had every advantage of us [women] in telling their own story. Education has been theirs in so much higher a degree; the pen has been in their hands."

None of the books Jane published in her lifetime included her name. There's speculation that pressure from her family — possibly her brother Edward's wealthy and socially prominent in-laws — induced Jane to remain "cloaked" in this way.

Jane Austen, Author

FROM ABOUT age twelve onward, Jane Austen tried her hand at all kinds of writing: stories, plays, poems, nonfiction, short novels. Carol Adams, Douglas Buchanan, and Kelly Gersch in their biography call the teen Jane Austen a "literary demolition expert": she took apart what she had read and experimented with putting it back together in playful, inventive ways. These were her first steps toward finding her own voice, her own style, as a writer.

This early work became known many years later as her "juvenilia." It's a lot of fun to read, and it's also shockingly good for such a young person. It's gleefully violent, filled with catastrophes and bad behavior, and, aside from spelling errors, it's stylistically sophisticated and confident – and hilarious.

Her sister Cassandra is thought to have been her first reader, and Jane also shared her work with her family, reading it aloud to them. Despite the fact that she wrote about all kinds of, well, unladylike things, the Austens seem to have been wonderfully supportive of the young writer. Besides, they loved to laugh.

It may have been during this time that Jane decided to write not just for fun, but to be published and in the hope of earning some money. (". . . tho' I like praise as well as anybody," she would later write about her career as an author, "I like what Edward calls *Pewter* too.") She loved novels about young women making their way in the world, and this is the type of book she decided to focus on – quite possibly a calculated decision that offered her the best chance to be published.

She wrote a short, glitteringly sharp novel called *Lady Susan* which apparently didn't meet with much enthusiasm from her family, and went on to write a longer, more conventionally romantic novel called *Elinor and Marianne*. It was followed swiftly by *First Impressions,* which she finished when she was only twenty-one. Her family applauded this bright, amusing love story, and her father even went so far as to send it to a London publisher on her behalf. It was curtly rejected, but Jane Austen kept writing anyway. When she was twenty-eight, she sold a funny, romantic manuscript called *Susan* to a different publisher, who failed to bring it out. It had to have been deeply frustrating to Jane – in fact, six years later she wrote an angry letter to the publisher – and, perhaps, a source of sadness and pain.

Yet despite these setbacks, and others, she seemed to maintain a deep faith in herself and her art. Several years after *First Impressions* had been turned down, Jane revised it, renamed it *Pride and Prejudice* (a phrase she liked from Fanny Burney's 1782 novel *Cecilia*), and saw it published. It has since become her most popular book.

Elinor and Marianne, renamed *Sense and Sensibility,* was her first published novel (1811), followed by *Pride and Prejudice* (1813), *Mansfield Park* (1814), and *Emma* (1815). Although she wrote anonymously, word was getting out about this talented, reclusive author, and she even began to — at last! — make some money. And how gratifying it must have been to learn that the Prince Regent, ruling Britain in the place of his incapacitated father King George III, admired her work. Not bad for a little country girl growing up in the middle of nowhere!

However, it was around this time, at the age of forty, that she began to feel seriously unwell and in 1816 she died, aged forty-one, possibly of cancer. No one knows for sure.

Susan, renamed *Northanger Abbey,* and another manuscript, *Persuasion,* were published a year after her death, and she left behind some uncompleted work as well.

Jane Austen's novels are, on one level, what we might think of as fairly conventional love stories, but they're also deeply concerned with an understanding of the self, the realities of money and class, and human nature. They were groundbreaking in how they portrayed intelligent women, whose mental and emotional capabilities provided them with a power that at the time may have been more fantasy than reality, but it was a revolutionary vision nonetheless. All this via writing that is witty, concise, and insightful, with a sparkling surface that can be very funny; underneath, sometimes difficult to perceive, are flickering currents of pathos and anger, suffusing Austen's work with a fascinating complexity.

The tragedy of her early death is immutable, but how satisfying, how thrilling, to bear witness to the maturation of that early, vulnerable bud of promise into a bloom of lasting brilliance.

TIMELINE

 1775

December 16

Jane Austen is born into a large family living in rural England. She is promptly nicknamed "Jenny."

 1776

April

At around four months of age, Jane is given into the care of a village woman, Nanny Littleworth.

1777

Summer

When Jane is about a year and a half old, she is brought home. Her siblings are James (nicknamed Jemmy; age twelve), George (age eleven), Edward (Neddy; ten), Henry (six), Cassandra (Cassy; five), and Francis (Frank; four).

George suffered from epilepsy and was likely both deaf and unable to speak. He was boarded nearby with a village family, possibly the Littleworths.

1779

Summer

Jane's brother Charles is born. He is the last of the eight Austen children.

At age fourteen, James goes to college in Oxford, fifty miles away, and eleven-year-old Edward accompanies wealthy older cousins Mr. and Mrs. Knight on a long journey.

Thirteen-year-old George is permanently boarded with a different family eight miles away.

1782

Winter

James and his brothers and friends stage the exciting melodrama *Matilda* in the family's dining parlor.

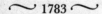

1783

Spring

Jane and Cassandra, ages seven and ten, along with their cousin Jane Cooper, age eleven, go to Oxford, where they attend school in the home of a relative, Mrs. Cawley.

September

The little school moves to the seaport of Southampton. All three girls fall ill; Jane Austen nearly dies. Thanks to plucky Jane Cooper, a letter is smuggled out and the girls' mothers promptly arrive. Jane and Cassandra go home with Mrs. Austen; Jane Cooper returns to Bath with her mother, who dies of the illness in October.

∼ 1784 ∼

Jane, eight, and Cassandra, eleven, are home this year.

Edward, sixteen, is formally adopted by Mr. and Mrs. Knight, and joins them at Godmersham, 100 miles away.

The Lefroy family moves into the neighborhood.

∼ 1785 ∼

August

Jane and Cassandra, ages nine and twelve, along with cousin Jane Cooper, age thirteen, attend the Abbey School in Reading, twenty miles from the Austen home.

～ 1786 ～

April

Francis, age eleven, goes to the naval academy in Portsmouth.

James (age twenty-one) and Edward (twenty) are, separately, touring Europe.

December

Jane and Cassandra, ages ten and thirteen, return home. Their formal education is now over. They are allowed use of the room adjoining their bedroom; they call it the Dressing Room.

Christmas

Glamorous Cousin Eliza, the Comtesse de Feuillide, visits.

～ 1787 ～

Scholars and biographers agree that this is the year when Jane Austen, age eleven, turning twelve, begins to write in a focused and inventive way.

SOURCES

A Companion to Jane Austen, edited by Claudia L. Johnston and Clara Tuite *✧* Wiley-Blackwell, 2012

A Goodly Heritage: A History of Jane Austen's Family by George Holbert Tucker *✧* Carcanet Press, 1984

A Jane Austen Education: How Six Novels Taught Me About Love, Friendship, and the Things That Really Matter by William Deresiewicz *✧* Penguin Press, 2011

A Jane Austen Household Book by Peggy Hickman *✧* David & Charles, 1997

A Portrait of Jane Austen by David Cecil *✧* Hill and Wang, 1979

All Things Austen: A Concise Encyclopedia of Austen's World by Kirstin Olsen *✧* Greenwood World Publishing, 2008

Becoming Jane: The Wit and Wisdom of Jane Austen, edited by Anne Newgarden *✧* Hyperion, 2007

Becoming Jane Austen by Jon Spence *✧* Hambledon Continuum, 2003

Creativity: Flow and the Psychology of Discovery and Invention by Mihaly Csikszentmihalyi *✧* HarperCollins Publishers, 1996

Desire and Domestic Fiction by Nancy Armstrong *✧* Oxford University Press, 1987

Emma by Jane Austen *✧* New American Library, 1964

"Give Your Ideas Some Legs: The Positive Effect of Walking on Creative Thinking" by Marily Oppezzo and Daniel L. Schwartz *✧* Stanford University, *Journal of Experimental Psychology: Learning, Memory, and Cognition,* Vol. 40, No. 4, 2014

Jane and Her Gentlemen: Jane Austen and the Men in Her Life and Novels by Audrey Hawkridge ❧ Peter Owen Publishers, 2000

Jane Austen by Carol Shields ❧ The Penguin Group, 2001

Jane Austen: A Life by David Nokes ❧ Farrar, Straus and Giroux, 1997

Jane Austen: A Life by Claire Tomalin, Vintage, 1999

Jane Austen: A Life Revealed by Catherine Reef ❧ Clarion Books, 2011

Jane Austen: Catherine and Other Writings, edited by Douglas Murray and Margaret Anne Doody ❧ Oxford University Press, 1993

Jane Austen: Her Life by Park Honan ❧ St. Martin's Press, 1987

Jane Austen: Woman and Writer by Joan Rees ❧ St. Martin's Press, 1976

Jane Austen the Woman: Some Biographical Insights by George Holbert Tucker ❧ St. Martin's Press, 1994

Jane Austen's Cults and Cultures by Claudia L. Johnson ❧ The University of Chicago Press, 2012

Jane Austen's England by Roy and Leslie Adkins ❧ Viking, 2013

Jane Austen's Letters, fourth edition, collected and edited by Deirde Le Faye ❧ Oxford University Press, 2011

Mansfield Park by Jane Austen ❧ Signet, 1984

Only a Novel: The Double Life of Jane Austen by Jane Aiken Hodge ❧ Coward, McCann & Geoghegan, 1972

Persuasion by Jane Austen ❧ Penguin Books, 1975

Please Understand Me II: Temperament, Character, Intelligence by David Keirsey ❧ Prometheus Nemesis Book Company, 1998

Presenting Miss Jane Austen by May Lamberton Becker ✦ Dodd, Mead and Company, 1952

Pride and Prejudice by Jane Austen ✦ Penguin Books, 1986

"Secrets of the Creative Brain" by Nancy C. Andreasen, *The Atlantic*, July/August, 2014

Sense and Sensibility by Jane Austen ✦ Penguin Books, 1995

The Age of Napoleon by Will and Ariel Durant ✦ Simon and Schuster, 1975

"The Aha! Moment" by Nessa Victoria Bryce ✦ *Scientific American*, July/August, 2014

The Bedside, Bathtub & Armchair Companion to Jane Austen by Carol Adams, Douglas Buchanan & Kelly Gesch ✦ The Continuum International Publishing Group, 2008

The Cambridge Introduction to Jane Austen by Janet Todd ✦ Cambridge University Press, 2006

The Creative Spirit by Daniel Goleman, Paul Kaufman, and Michael Ray ✦ Dutton, 1992

The English: A Social History 1066 – 1945 by Christopher Hibbert ✦ W.W. Norton & Company, 1987

The Friendly Jane Austen by Natalie Tyler ✦ Viking, 1999

The Jane Austen Companion, edited by J. David Grey, A. Walton Litz, and Brian Southam ✦ Macmillan Publishing Company, 1986

The Real Jane Austen: A Life in Small Things by Paula Byrne ✦ HarperCollins Publishers, 2013

The World of Jane Austen by Nigel Nicolson ✦ Orion Publishing Group, 1997

What Matters in Jane Austen? Twenty Crucial Puzzles Solved by John Mullan ✦ Bloomsbury Press, 2013

Why Jane Austen? by Rachel M. Brownstein ✦ Columbia University Press, 2011

101 Things You Didn't Know about Jane Austen by Patrice Hannon, Ph.D. ✦ Adams Media, 2007

About the Illustrations

In an Internet-dominated world with access to what may well be literally an infinite number of whimsical cat pictures, it is a hard and painful fact that there are at present only two verifiable images of Jane Austen.

Both of them show Jane as an adult, and both were rendered by her sister Cassandra. One is a watercolor of Jane at twenty-seven, sitting out of doors and looking out into the distance, her face entirely shielded by her bonnet.

The other is a pencil and watercolor sketch in which Jane, age thirty-five, sits facing the viewer, although her gaze is turned away. Her arms are crossed and her expression is somber, pensive, even a little sour.

Over the years, various Austen family members, friends, and acquaintances offered descriptions that today combine to create an *idea* of a tall, thin woman who had sparkling hazel eyes, a round face and a rosy complexion, high cheekbones, and curly brown hair.

It wasn't much to go on.

Given the extreme paucity of source material, both for how Jane looked as a child and what her surroundings were like, the illustrations for this book, which show Jane from birth until age twelve, can most accurately be described as impressionistic. They are guesses only; but they are offered in the hope of providing a sense of — a feeling for — young Jane Austen and the world in which she lived.

ACKNOWLEDGEMENTS

With many thanks to, and deep appreciation for, these friends, family members, and colleagues, whose categories overlap in a way that makes me feel very fortunate:

Robert Bernstein
Nancy Cleary
Carol Deaktor
Kate Griggs
Rachael Ignatoff
Eric Jensen
Toni Jensen
Belinda Mulliken
Laura Ross
Leslie Ruder
Irene Skolnick
Steve Wineman

–LP

ABOUT THE AUTHOR AND ILLUSTRATOR

Lisa Pliscou graduated from Harvard University with an honors degree in English and American Literature and Language. Writing for both adults and children, she's the author of several other books including *Higher Education* and *Dude*. Her work has been praised by the *Wall Street Journal,* the *Los Angeles Times, Publishers Weekly, The Horn Book, Booklist,* the Associated Press, and other media.

Lisa lives in northern California with her family. You can connect with her via her website, www.LisaPliscou.com.

Originally from Berkshire County, **Massimo Mongiardo** received a BFA from the Massachusetts College of Art and Design and now lives in New York City. In addition to illustrating and designing books for both children and adults, he's worked on a wide range of other projects including magazine illustration, concept and character design for theater and film productions, and design and illustration for skateboards, posters, and apparel.

His website is www.MassimoMongiardo.com.

163

INDEX

A

Abbey School, 59–60, 63, 109, 118–120, 121–122,155
Adams, Carol, 149
Adkins, Leslie, 84
Adkins, Roy, 84
All Things Austen (Olsen), 92
Andreasen, Nancy C., 100, 101, 103–104, 131
Antoinette, Marie, 63, 121
Aristotle, 103
Armstrong, Nancy, 133, 147
Auchincloss, Louis, xi
Austen, Cassandra (Cassy; sister), 8, 11, 15, 23, 31, 35–36, 43–44, 47, 51, 59, 67–68, 75, 85, 87, 89–91, 94–95, 99, 102, 107, 108–110, 112, 114, 118, 122, 126–128, 133, 134–135, 143, 146, 149, 153, 154, 155, 156, 161
Austen, Charles (brother), 35, 36, 102, 126–127, 154
Austen, Edward (Neddy; brother), 7, 15, 35–36, 55, 67, 85, 89–90, 102–103, 110, 115–116, 126–127, 145, 148, 150, 153, 154, 155, 156
Austen, Francis (Frank; brother), 7, 15, 67, 85, 89–91, 126–127, 153, 156
Austen, George (brother), 7, 35–36, 43–44, 85, 90, 102–104, 108, 153, 154
Austen, Henry (brother), 7, 15, 67, 85, 89–90, 107, 116, 153
Austen, James (Jemmy; brother), 7, 15, 35–36, 39–40, 44, 67, 85, 89–90, 98, 102–103, 105, 106, 107, 108, 109, 126–127, 153, 154, 156
Austen, Jane (works)
  Elinor and Marianne, 150, 151
  Emma, 82, 98, 111, 116, 119–120, 151
  First Impressions, 150
  Lady Susan, 150
  Love and Freindship, 113
  Mansfield Park, 82, 98, 107, 109–110, 116, 122, 127, 132, 151

  Northanger Abbey, vii, 82, 92, 98, 119, 131, 132, 151
  Persuasion, 82, 110, 114, 116–117, 125, 127, 148, 151
  Pride and Prejudice, 82, 84, 92, 95, 98, 110, 116, 117, 122, 124, 132, 135, 150, 151
  Sense and Sensibility, 82, 98, 109, 110–111, 119–120, 122, 132, 151
  Susan, 150, 151
Austen, Mr. (Papa; father), 7, 11, 15–16, 23, 27, 31, 35–36, 40, 43, 55, 59, 67–68, 83, 85, 87–88, 89–91, 94–95, 97, 99–100, 102, 105, 108–110, 115, 118–119, 126, 128, 132, 135, 145, 150
Austen, Mrs. (Mama; mother), 3, 7, 11, 15, 23, 31, 35–36, 39–40, 43, 51, 59, 67, 75, 83, 85–86, 87, 89–91, 94–95, 99, 102–103, 105–107, 108–110, 114, 118–119, 126, 128, 134–135, 145, 155

B

Balls, 63, 75, 114, 121, 134, 135
Bath, 110, 111, 113, 114, 119, 155
Bennet, Elizabeth (character), 92, 95, 117, 122, 135
Bennet, Mr. (character), 94–95, 135
Bennet, Mrs. (character), 84, 135
Bertram, Edmund (character), 98, 132
Bertrams (characters), 110, 116
Bible, the, 23, 94
Bigg-Wither, Harris, 124, 146
Bingley, Miss (character), 84
Birth, 3, 83–84, 146
Boarders (Mr. Austen's students), 15–16, 31, 43, 68, 71–72, 75, 89, 90, 91, 99, 108, 126, 128
Books, 31–32, 36, 48, 55, 56, 64, 71, 79, 84, 96, 99, 100, 102, 112, 115–116, 121, 123, 127, 130–133, 134, 137, 141, 142, 147–148, 150–151
Bourdieu, Pierre, 95
Brain, and the creative process, 100–101, 103–104, 128–129

Brandon, Colonel (character), 122
Brunton, Mary, 148
Bryce, Nessa Victoria, 128–129
Buchanan, Douglas, 149
Burney, Fanny, 150
Byrne, Paula, 103, 110, 132

C

Campbell family (characters), 116
Cawley, Mrs. Ann, 43, 47–48, 75, 108–
   109, 112–113, 119, 134, 154
Cecil, David, 94
Cecilia (Burney), 150
Chawton, 110
Childrearing, 85–86
Chores, 15, 36, 89–90, 99, 102
Churchill, Frank (character), 116
Cinderella, 100, 123
Class, social, 100, 116, 120, 144–145, 151
Clergymen, 98
Collins, Mr. (character), 98, 117
Colonies, the, 23, 94
Comte de Feuillide (count), 63, 121–123
Comtesse de Feuillide. *See* de Feuillide,
   Eliza
Conduct books, 133
Cooper, Dr. Edward (uncle), 114
Cooper, Jane (aunt), 51, 75, 114, 134, 155
Cooper, Jane (cousin), 43, 47, 51, 108,
   112–113, 114, 118, 154, 155
Crawford, Mary (character), 116, 122
Creative Spirit, The (Gardner), 137–138
Creativity, 93, 95, 100, 101, 103–104,
   128–129, 131–132, 135–136, 137–138,
   143
*Creativity: Flow and the Psychology of Discovery
   and Invention* (Csikszentmihalyi), 95–96,
   104
Csikszentmihalyi, Mihaly, 95–96, 104,
   131–132, 135–136, 143
Culhams, the, 103
Cultural capital, 95–96

D

Dancing, 64, 101, 121
Darcy, Fitzwilliam (character), 84, 132
Dashwood, Elinor (character), 110–111,
   132–133

Dashwood, Marianne (character), 132–
   133
de Feuillide, Eliza (cousin), 63–64, 75, 107,
   121–123, 134, 156
Death, 51, 84, 110, 114, 151, 152, 155
Desire and Domestic Fiction (Armstrong),
   133, 147
Dickens, Charles, 93
Doody, Margaret Anne, 97–98, 135
Dressing Room, the, 68, 126–129, 156
Dryden, John, 104

E

Edison, Thomas, 138
Ehrlich, Gretel, 93
Einstein, Albert, 137
Elinor and Marianne (Austen), 150, 151. *See
   also Sense and Sensibility* (Austen)
Eliza (characters), 122
Elliot, Anne (character), 114, 116–117,
   125, 127, 148
Elliot, William (character), 125
Elton, Mr. (character), 98
Elton, Mrs. (character), 111
Emma (Austen), 82, 98, 111, 116, 119–120,
   151
Exercise, and creativity, 92–93

F

Fairfax, Jane (character), 116
Faulkner, William, vii, viii
Ferrars, Edward (character), 98
Ferrars, Robert (character), 110
First Impressions (Austen), 150
Fordyce, 98
Formal speech, influence of, 97
Frontal lobe, role in the creative process,
   101

G

Gardner, Howard, 137–138
Gersch, Kelly, 149
Goddard, Mrs. (character), 119
Godmersham, 55, 115–116, 155
Goodly Heritage, A (Tucker), 86
Grandison, Sir Charles (character), 55,
   71–72, 115, 130

H

Hackitt, Sarah (Madame La Tournelle), 59, 118–119
Hampshire, 83
Hannon, Patrice, 107
Hastings (cousin), 122
History of Little Goody Two-Shoes, The, 100
Hodge, Jane Aiken, 86, 91
Home, 11, 36, 87–88, 108–111
Home theatricals, 39, 106–107, 154
Honan, Park, 87, 109, 120

I

Idealist personality, 123–124
India, 23, 63, 94, 121, 122
Iowa Writers Workshop, 103

J

Jane Austen: A Life (Nokes), 114
Jane Austen: A Life (Tomalin), 83, 91, 106, 109
Jane Austen: Her Life (Honan), 87–88, 109, 120
Jane Austen Companion, The (Doody), 97–98, 135
Jane Austen's England (Adkins and Adkins), 84
"Jane Austen's Reading" (Doody), 135

K

Kalman, Maira, 93
Keirsey, David, 123–124
King, Stephen, 93
King George III, 151
Knight, Fanny (niece), 142, 146
Knight, Mr. and Mrs. (cousins), 35, 36, 55, 102, 115, 154, 155

L

Lady Susan (Austen), 150
La Tournelle, Madame. *See* Hackitt, Sarah
Laughter, 11, 23, 39, 47, 59–60, 64, 72, 76, 87, 90, 94, 95, 105, 112, 118, 121, 130, 132, 134, 142, 149
Leaving home, 35–36, 43–44, 67, 102–103, 108–111, 115–116, 126–127, 154, 155

L

Lefroy, Madam, 56, 71, 75, 115–117, 130, 134
Lefroy, Tom, 117, 145
Lefroys (neighbors), 56, 115, 155
Littleworth, Nanny, 7–8, 11, 35, 85, 87, 90, 102, 153
London, 63, 121
Love and Freindship (Austen), 113
Lucas, Charlotte (character), 117

M

Mansfield Park (Austen), 82, 98, 107, 109–110, 116, 122, 127, 132, 151
Matilda, 39, 105, 154
Memoir of Jane Austen, 83
Mental illness, 103–104
Middle names, lack of, 84
Midsummer Night's Dream, A (Shakespeare), 104
Morland, Catherine (character), vii, 92, 119

N

Naming, of children, 3, 83–84, 153
Neurophysiology, in studying creativity and the brain, 101
Neuroscience, in studying creativity, genetics, and mental illness, 103–104
Nietzsche, Friedrich, 93
Nokes, David, 114
Northanger Abbey (Austen), vii, 82, 92, 98, 119, 131, 132, 151. *See also Susan* (Austen)
Novel(s), 51, 71, 72, 82, 98, 109, 113, 114, 117, 120, 122, 130–132, 141, 147–148, 149, 150, 151–152

O

Oates, Joyce Carol, 93
Olsen, Kirstin, 92
101 Things You Didn't Know about Jane Austen (Hannon), 107
Only a Novel: The Double Life of Jane Austen (Hodge), 86
Oxford, 35, 43, 47, 67, 90, 102, 103, 108, 109, 112, 126, 154

P

Palmer, Charlotte (character), 120

Parietal lobe, role in the creative process, 101

Persuasion (Austen), 82, 110, 114, 116–117, 125, 127, 148, 151

Philadelphia (cousin), 122

Play, 19, 35, 36, 92, 102

Please Understand Me II: Temperament, Character, Intelligence (Keirsey), 123–124

Portrait of Jane Austen, A (Cecil), 94

Portsmouth, 67, 126, 156

Poverty, 43, 108–109, 116, 145–146

Practical Education, 127, 147

Price, Fanny (character), 109–110, 116

Pride and Prejudice (Austen), 82, 84, 92, 95, 98, 110, 116, 117, 122, 124, 132, 135, 150, 151

Prince Regent, the, 151

Proposal, marriage, 117, 124, 146

Q

Queen Elizabeth, 71, 130

R

Reading, 16, 23, 32, 36, 55, 68, 71–72, 75, 89, 91, 94, 99, 102, 115–116, 123, 126–129, 130–131, 134–135, 147–148, 149

Reading (city), 119, 155

Reality Hunger (Shields), vii

Rector, Mr. Austen as, 27, 35, 97, 102

Revolution, French, 123

Robinson Crusoe, 91, 127

Rowling, J.K., 93

Russell, Lady (character), 116

S

School, 35, 43, 47–48, 59–60, 67, 95, 102–103, 108–109, 112, 118–120, 121, 122, 126, 154, 155, 156

"Secrets of the Creative Brain" (Andreasen), 100

Sense and Sensibility (Austen), 82, 98, 109, 110–111, 119–120, 122, 132, 151. *See also Elinor and Marianne* (Austen)

Sermons to Young Women (Fordyce), 98

Servants, 15, 89, 91

Shakespeare, 101, 104

Shaw, George Bernard, xi

Shields, Carol, 92, 107, 111, 135

Shields, David, vii

Sickness, 47–48, 51, 92, 106, 112–113, 114, 151, 155

Social class, 116, 120, 144–145

Southampton, 47, 51, 112–113, 114, 155

St. John's College, 103

Steventon, 83–84, 110, 111, 119

Stuart, Mary, 71, 130

Sunday, 27, 97–98

Susan (Austen), 150, 151. *See also Northanger Abbey* (Austen)

Susan, Lady (character), 122

T

Temporal association cortices, role in the creative process, 101

Terman, Lewis M., 100

Theatricals, 106–107, 154

Thoreau, Henry David, 93

Tilney, Henry (character), 98

Tom (uncle), 103

Tomalin, Claire, 83, 85–86, 91, 106, 109, 116

Tracts, religious, 97–98

Tucker, George Herbert, 86

Typhus, 113

W

Walking, 92–93

Wentworth, Frederick (character), 117

West Indies, 23, 94

Whitman, Walt, 93

Willoughby (character), 122

Woolf, Virginia, 93

Wordsworth, William, 93

Writing, 39–40, 56, 67, 71, 75–76, 79, 84, 105–107, 115, 127–129, 130–132, 134–135, 137, 141, 149–152, 156

Y

Young Ladies Instructor, The, 72, 130

CPSIA information can be obtained
at www.ICGtesting.com
Printed in the USA
LVOW05s0704081215
465839LV00011B/12/P